Dr. Joan Freeman is the author of many books and scientific papers on the development of children's abilities, which have won her widespread acclaim. She received her doctorate in Child Psychology from the University of Manchester, and lectures frequently at universities and conferences throughout the world.

She has been awarded the honour of a Fellowship of the British Psychological Society, and has been elected first President of the European Council for High Ability (ECHA), an association which covers Europe from Moscow to Naples. It promotes the development of talent during the whole life span.

Joan Freeman is married to a psychiatrist and they have four grown-up children, three boys and a girl, who are respectively a computer scientist/musician, a musician, a builder, and a mathematician.

BRIGHT AS A BUTTON

HOW TO ENCOURAGE YOUR CHILDREN'S TALENTS

Dr. Joan Freeman

Cartoons by Willow

An OPTIMA book

©JOAN FREEMAN 1991
© Illustrations by WILLOW 1991

First published in 1991 by
Macdonald Optima, a division of
Macdonald & Co. (Publishers) Ltd

A member of Maxwell Macmillan Publishing Corporation

British Library Cataloguing in Publication Data

Freeman, Joan
  Bright as a button.
  I. Title
  649

    ISBN 0–356–19671–2

Macdonald & Co. (Publishers) Ltd
165 Great Dover Street
London SE1 4YA

Typeset in Century Schoolbook by Leaper & Gard Ltd, Bristol

Printed and bound in Great Britain by
The Guernsey Press Co. Ltd, Guernsey, Channel Islands.

CONTENTS

ACKNOWLEDGMENTS

In developing my ideas, I have been greatly helped by the work of countless child psychologists who have described their research in academic journals and books; I have searched through these statistics (not to mention the jargon) and translated their discoveries into practical everyday ideas. I have also included findings from my own research, in particular the 15-year Gulbenkian research project that I directed on children growing into young adults, whose abilities ranged from average to gifted. Overall, I found that those who made the greatest progress in developing their potential came from the most educationally positive homes, where they received the mental freedom, encouragement and opportunities they needed, whatever their abilities. The children and their parents who took part in the project have taught me more than they knew, and I thank them sincerely.

I would also like to express my appreciation to the many people, parents, teachers in all kinds of education, and students, who have spent time discussing children and their abilities with me while I have been writing this book. It has always been worthwhile to hear their comments and to compare their experiences with my own.

My thanks go to WordPerfect UK Ltd., for their superb word processing programme which has made my life very much easier. Harriet Griffey, my editor at Optima has been a generous source of support and encouragement, and I thank her sincerely. And to my husband, Hugh, whose eagle eye spotted many a clumsy sentence and stray comma as the book took shape, thank you.

Joan Freeman
London 1991

1
INTRODUCTION

Parents are the best-placed people to help their children fulfil their potentials. Indeed, there has never been a better time for a child to be growing to peak ability. With the breaking down of old social and political barriers, ability is at a premium. The pursuit of individual excellence is a choice available to everyone, from all walks of life. Every child wants to be good at something, and every child can be. Bright children, lucky enough to be born to loving, concerned and understanding parents, have the very best chance of developing their minds with pleasure and success. Parenting is an art and, like all artists, parents need guidance and practice in developing their sensitivity and skill. This book, written from a sound basis of scientific knowledge, is devoted to helping them.

The psychological foundations for learning start to be

laid down at birth, and are already fairly stable by the time a child is three years old. Of course, there is still plenty of time for mental growth and change after that, and although no single method of bringing up children can be sure to work, even for those in the same family, some methods do seem to be more worthwhile than others. Many of the best are set out here.

Probably the most effective way parents can help their children to grow to maturity and strength is by forming a loving, accepting and supporting relationship with them from the day they are born. This must not be suffocating and smothering, but rather should provide a warm cradle leading to a lively intelligence that will last for life. Although babies develop basic physical skills without help, such as reaching out for things, parents can encourage them to enjoy experimenting with their new learning. Even for a tiny baby, variety is the spice of life.

The deep pleasure that a baby finds in adventures in early learning will do a lot to help her feel confident about the lifetime of learning ahead, and this will continue to help her as she discovers her own special strengths and interests. Doing the right thing with your child at the right time will give her greater confidence, followed by an easier educational climb, than she could ever have gained without your help.

If you can enhance your child's inborn ability by encouraging her sense of self-worth, it will allow her to make full use of the gifts she was born with. Though the finer practical details of guiding the intellectual progress of bright lively children is started at home, it is continued by teachers. One of the most welcome benefits of the educational interest that is now being taken in helping bright children, both at home and in school, is the effect this has on all children. In schools where bright children are encouraged, all pupils can feel important and valuable, while teaching takes on a fresh sparkle.

This book offers a positive and practical psychological approach to children's intellectual development – an approach very much more concerned with 'dos' than 'don'ts'. It contains a minimum of what your child should be doing at any particular age – lively minded children don't always stick to the rules. Instead, it draws on a wide collection of research-based knowledge about how children's minds develop and work, with suggestions about what parents can do to help them along.

As you become familiar with this positive approach, it will become a habit. You and your children will then be better able to grow together, learning from each other. Perhaps my own greatest joy in parenting has not been in what I have taught my four children, but what I have learned from them. They certainly led me into areas of interest that I didn't even know existed before.

The famous child psychiatrist Donald Winnicott once said that you don't have to be a perfect parent – just good enough. This thought has given me comfort over the years of my own children's upbringing. I pass his words on to you, in the sincere hope that you too will find comfort in them, as well as great pleasure in the time you share with your children.

Finally, I have chosen to use 'he' or 'she' more or less alternately in describing babies and children. The reason for this is simply because that is the way boys and girls are born – more or less alternately. As parents too come in both sexes, I have only referred to mother or father specifically where this is important. In general, I am writing about activities and relationships between parents and children which apply equally, whoever is doing the parenting.

2
BRIGHT AND LIVELY

The world needs children who are bright as buttons, and who will keep their sparkle as they go through life – those whose potential capabilities could contribute greatly to life in all fields of endeavour and in every corner of the world, if only they were given the chance to develop them. The bright child may be yours or mine, whether we are rich or poor, whatever our beliefs and wherever we live. At least one in ten children – millions around the world – are born bright enough to make them quite outstanding in some way. And remember that half of all babies born are above average.

What people see as especially valuable in children's

abilities depends to some extent on their own point of view and on the lives they lead. The most valued cave-boy, for example, would probably have been the best prospective hunter, with a keen sense of where animals might be found. In Ancient Greece a bright girl might have been noticed for her logical thinking. By the turn of this century a bright child was expected to recite long passages of text from memory, clearly and with expression, or write columns of figures in long straight lines; hard work, obeying the rules and coming top of the class were the mark of potential success. Robert Graves, the poet, in his autobiography *Goodbye to All That*, described how his father took him out of school when he found his son in tears over a 23-times multiplication table. Graves also recalled having to do mental arithmetic to the rhythm of a metronome.

Now we recognise that for all children, it is not only what they produce (or reproduce) that makes their work valuable, but the touch of lively imagination they show. This need is obvious not only in the arts, but also in the sciences. Einstein was very bored in his German grammar school, where he was expected to reproduce what he had been taught, and he didn't do at all well in school exams. Then, when his uncle taught him how to use his imagination with numbers, he went on to change the world of mathematics and physics.

Einstein, it is true, was a genius, one of those rare people who bring brand new ideas into being. Geniuses are rather more than just super-clever or even highly gifted; they are truly great people who leave their society, and perhaps even the world, a little different because of their contribution. Beethoven, Picasso, Isaac Newton, Marie Curie were all geniuses. Even as little children they had shown unusually strong interest in the special subject areas that later came to dominate their lives, sometimes to the exclusion of most other things. In a study of eminent scientists in America in the 1950s, Anne Roe found that very early in their childhoods her scientists-to-be had made serious adult-like collections and had devised and carried out experiments by themselves.

This ability of a genius to be original, to push back the

frontiers of knowledge and ideas, is often seen very early in life. Mozart was composing at the age of 4, Mendelssohn at 9 and Handel at 11. Alexander Pope had poems published by the age of 12, as did Françoise Sagan, and Robert Burns by 14. When Henry Ford started as a watch repairer he was so young that his employers found it better for him not to be seen by customers at his workbench.

This book is written for the parents of children who will never be considered geniuses, except in very rare instances, but who are all bright and talented in some way. Of course, most parents of bright children want them to lead happy, normal lives, and so I have brought together my experience as a psychologist, teacher and parent to help them understand and encourage their children to do their best and be happy. Parents are the best resource a bright child has; they are the most sensitive to their children's needs and the most concerned about their futures.

CHILDREN'S NORMAL INTELLECTUAL DEVELOPMENT

Psychologists are never very willing to commit themselves to saying exactly what a child ought to be doing at any particular age. This is because there is such a wide variation between the ways that individual children develop. Both physically and psychologically, a child may either grow in spurts, with rests in between, or else keep on growing steadily. Every child has his own tempo and style, as personal as his face.

Most parents, however, would like some understanding of normal development in children, in order to see how their own compare. But what is called normal really means average. The 'normal' developmental levels are actually averages taken from the measurement of thousands of children of the same age. Yet even averages can change with changing conditions. Intelligence levels, for example, are going up steadily, especially in countries where the food supply had been poor but has now improved. Furthermore, averages are not easily transferable from one national culture to another; what is encouraged in one, such as asking questions in America, might be inhibited in another such as Sweden, where the ability to be silent is respected.

However, bearing all this in mind, what follows is an outline of progress in a normal child's mental development. There is more detail about the way the mind works and how you can help in Chapter 5.

Using words

A newborn baby will listen and respond to words and signs. By a year old a baby will have learned to produce a few words herself, like 'Mama' and 'Dada'. In between trying them out, she will practise her new talking skills by babbling. It is sometimes hard to tell when a baby has started to use new words because parents often understand the meaning behind baby's sounds before they become recognisable to other people. However, here are some guidelines that psychologists use to see whether a baby is beginning to speak:

- A baby should somehow indicate that she understands the meaning of the sound, like saying 'Dada' and pointing to or looking at her father.
- A baby should use the word at different times in the same way, and use it spontaneously, not just in immediate imitation of someone else.
- A word should be clear enough for other adults to understand, at least when they are tuned in to what the baby is trying to say.

Most babies can manage a few short sentences by the time they are two years old, such as 'Daddy go car'. Girls are usually in advance of boys in the use of words, both in number of words and in forming sentences. Wide-ranging research in America, directed by Eleanor Maccoby, has shown that not only do girls say their first word earlier, but they go on to talk properly earlier. Boys usually (but not always) catch up in later childhood.

You can count up the number of words your child already has, to see how well she's getting on, though late talking doesn't automatically mean slow mental development, either now or in the future. Winston Churchill didn't talk until he was three years old, although most children of that age would have a vocabulary of up to 900 words. It is normal, too, for children who are learning to speak to forget some of the words you thought they knew, and to have to learn them again.

Learning to talk is affected by a number of things in a toddler's life, such as his need to communicate by that particular means. For example, if as parents you manage to interpret your baby's needs for food and drink by means of his gestures, then he might be a little slow in getting round to asking for them by name. But this doesn't matter in the long run.

Learning to talk is linked to emotion, too, so that children who have had upsets in their lives – perhaps moving house, or a change of people who look after them – may suffer a setback in talking. The way children feel about words also affects the way they use them and the thoughts that go with them. This is true for adults too, though it's hard to pinpoint it exactly because so many of those feelings are buried deep in our unconscious minds. We are rarely aware of the way we talk and think; we just get on with it.

Using numbers

It may be hard to believe, but future computational skills have their roots in the first year of life. By the time she's a year old a baby can put one brick on top of another on a smooth firm surface. In this way she begins to glimpse the basic arithmetical idea of 'more than' and 'less than', which will be clear by about two years old. An average three year old can usually count to five, and by four years old to ten. But a real understanding of numbers only comes after they are memorised. To a toddler the number 4 is not the abstract idea of the cipher 4 that older children understand; it depends on practical counting. But by the age of three a toddler can usually cope with ideas of 'enoughness', which is somewhere between saying the numbers and understanding them. You should try asking your toddler 'Have I put enough cups on the table for tea?' to see how far she's come.

By the time she's five years old a bright child is probably able to add numbers up to five, and by six years old she may not only be able to add numbers up to ten, but also to subtract numbers under five. To start with boys and girls seem to develop at an even pace in arithmetical skills, but then boys are often found to do better on spatial skills, which shows up in ability to draw patterns and understand how mechanical things work. What we don't know, though, is how much of that skill is native inclination, and how much is due to the different forms of encouragement that each sex gets in these matters.

Using memory

From about the age of ten most people find it almost impossible to remember anything that happened to them as babies and toddlers. Freud called it 'infantile amnesia', and said it was due to our repression of things we don't want to remember. But recent psychological studies have given a much more straightforward explanation, and one that offers the means to help little children use their memories more effectively; this is a vital part of their learning process.

The early problems children have in memorising are due to their inefficient methods of sorting and storing their experiences; this is simply because they are still experimenting with ways of doing it. In order to remember, that is to bring what you have experienced to the front of your mind, there has to be some sort of mental organisation from which it can be taken. We do this with 'headings' or triggers, which identify the memory via familiar pathways of thought. The difficulty in getting back to very early images is because the organisational set-up was simply not available at that time, so the memories remain unsorted and inaccessible later.

You can see this in action with toddlers, who may find it difficult to remember what they did even the day before.

You can help a child get his memorising structure working by using careful detailed questioning which links up different parts of a story, so that even two year olds can make a better showing. This is most effectively done by actually being in the same place as the event you are asking the child about. For example, 'What did Grandma give you to eat yesterday?' will produce a better response if it is asked at Grandma's house, not at home.

Another real problem you have to recognise is that very young children don't always have the words to explain themselves adequately. One way out of this is to let them act out their memories, such as taking them to the same playground as the previous day and ask them to demonstrate what they remember. Or you could tell the child part of a story, stopping at several points, and encouraging him to fill in the missing bits.

Helping a little one to make better use of what he already has can take a lot of perseverance, but, like all exercises, practice improves the action. After all, it's the children with the most efficient methods of remembering who can get swiftly into the knowledge they already possess, and also use those methods to add to that knowledge.

Using experience

Some kinds of mental development need experience. The concept of time, for example, calls for memories of past events, as well as some language ability. Toddlers can usually begin to plan ahead with the idea of time by the age of three. They can be encouraged to start planning using something they know well, such as bedtime or teatime.

Unlike adults, though, little children will not yet have accumulated the experience with which to cope with new situations. A baby, for example, has to learn from many fun demonstrations that Daddy's face is going to reappear over the top of the chair when they're playing peek-a-boo. Later on, the game loses its excitement when she knows he's crouching down there all the time. At about a year old, a crawling baby can watch you put a toy under a cushion and he'll 'find' it again. But if you pretend to put it under one cushion and sneak it under another one instead, he'll still only look under the first. He hasn't enough experience to realise that, if it's not under the first one, it may be under another. He should be able to cope with more than one hiding place, though, by the time he's 18 months old.

A little child also needs experience before she can learn to reason. It takes at least three years to work up a recognisable level of argument which involves real responses and not just statements of opinions. By five years old a child is usually able to draw sensible conclusions from, and to discuss the differences and similarities between, what she sees. You may remember that Christopher Robin was about five years old when he could compare Nanny's dressing gown ('a beautiful blue, but it hasn't a hood') with his own ('Mine has a hood').

Sometimes little ones lack the knowledge of social convention which they need in order to reach the 'right' conclusions; for example, a toddler may want to marry Mummy or Daddy when he or she grows up. They may also fail to work things out carefully enough; they haven't got the patience to negotiate paths of reasoning, so instead jump to logical (but incorrect) solutions. For example, taking his cue from adults, one of our children used to get a 'heggache' in his tummy when he was small; nothing wrong with his thinking or logical interpretation, and fortunately easy to understand.

Using letters
Sometime during toddlerhood children discover that making scribbles on paper is a fun way of expressing their thoughts and feelings. Then, through copying shapes and drawing pictures, many can shape a few letters by the time they are four. But many only start doing this at school, when they are five. Reading and writing often progress together at the beginning of school, though when children really love reading, their writing can lag behind.

Most children learn to read when they go to school, and can manage picture books with simple sentences by the end of their first year there. Some very bright ones, though, seem to teach themselves to read by absorbing words from all around, such as on cereal packets, road signs and record labels. A clever child may even recognise the meaning of familiar three-letter words by the age of three, and may recognise his own name if you print it out in big letters (depending on how difficult a name it is).

The age by which children learn to use letters in reading and writing depends a lot on the encouragement and assistance they receive at home. If you, as a parent, enjoy using words yourself, then you can expect that your child will too.

KEEPING A DIARY

Deciding whether your child is bright, and how and when to give her the right kind of attention, requires careful observation. For this, it can be very helpful to keep a diary, though it may sound like a bit of a chore. But, often, when you put something in writing, it helps you to take a step outside the hurly-burly of everyday living so that you can get a clearer, more objective, view of what is happening in your family. Then, looking back, you may be able to see how situations have developed, and how they can be altered. A diary will not only help you to judge whether you have a bright child – for example, whether she was always intellectually advanced for her age – but, of equal importance, it will help you to watch her emotional development. As intellectual and emotional development are tied together, they should be watched together.

Your record book doesn't have to be a proper printed diary, and you don't even have to write in it regularly: simply keep it handy, so that you can jot down things as they happen or when you particularly feel like it. A small notebook is perfect, preferably with a hard cover so that it will last well through many readings, and maybe several children, over the years. It may be the best book you've ever read.

There are three aspects of diary-keeping to keep in mind when you're writing about your child's development:

- Progress.
- Feelings.
- Plans.

However, it is more advantageous if, when you write, you try to think through the events that occur, rather than just keeping a record. For example, instead of writing 'Mary's back teeth through. Bill (husband) away this week', try to make your entry more like this:

Mary's back teeth showing with much crying. Bill's been away a week now. Is it pain she's crying for, or can she be missing him? I know that I am. Can I be passing my misery on to Mary? I'll keep closer to her and take her out for a change of scene this afternoon.

Any interpretation you choose to give to the events in your life is up to you. But it's your opinion that counts in your family, and diaries are supposed to be private.

Try to take a long view of your child's development, both when you're writing and when you're reading through your diary. It can help you to see changing patterns in development. Perhaps you will be able to see how right you were when you thought Richard was trying to talk at six months old and you were told that you were an over-ambitious mother, or maybe it becomes plain how his early self-confidence took a dip when he started school. A diary can help you to see things in perspective, and may help to spot potential problems before they have a chance to become entrenched. After some years you might find you have built up a useful series of entries, like the following ones about how Sarah started learning to read.

Eight months old Showed Sarah the pictures in her board book. She reached out for it and showed real interest. Am very excited, so's Robert. Mother says Sarah's still far too young to read.

One year and two months Sarah can turn the pages of her new cloth book and frowns over the pictures. She pretends to be reading; well, I think so. Lots of fun, we laugh a lot. It gives her great pleasure and it gives me pleasure too to watch her.

Three years and four months Now that she can read a few words, Sarah seems very keen to learn more. She's driving me mad with 'What's this, and this?' I can't cope with her demands and the new baby. Sometimes I can give her the hug I know she needs, but I seem so cross nowadays.

Four years old Sarah's started nursery school. Feel great relief, but she screamed the place down. Should have prepared her better. Robert's work has let up a bit, so I hope he'll spend more time with her. Wish I could too.

Five years old Proper school, but Sarah doesn't seem very keen. Teacher says she's clever, but won't try. Worried. Robert and I must try to give her a lot of love and support every day. She really needs us now.

Six years old Sarah on an even course at school: glad I kept a diary.

From time to time, describe a typical day in the life of your child. Does it seemed balanced to you? Does she have to spend all the time doing things that only interest you? Perhaps you could offer her a little more choice. Are you providing enough praise and encouragement to build up her confidence to explore? Find out what children usually do at this age; you could discover that your expectations are too high, and such knowledge could avoid imminent collision between your expectations and her achievement. Your diary is really your personal textbook of your child's total development. Try to develop a feeling for her character, at the same time as watching out for any special talents.

DO YOU THINK YOUR CHILD MAY BE SPECIALLY CLEVER?

Parents are the most likely people to spot a clever child; after all, they've had longer than anyone else to get to know

him. Sometimes they judge by watching him play with
other children and noticing how he's ahead of them in, say,
asking more penetrating questions, or discovering how to
do things more quickly. Sometimes parents just feel it in
their bones, as a sort of hunch; such intuition can often be
reliable, and should be investigated further. However, it is
not normally necessary to have a child tested by an
educational psychologist: using the ideas in this book may
well be enough.

How to spot a clever toddler

The old physical milestones – when a child first sits up,
crawls, stands up, or walks – are no longer seen as such
firm indicators of intellectual potential as they used to be.
Mental characteristics are really a much better guide,
though they're not entirely reliable because children can
change incredibly quickly. Clever children are just as
different from one another as any other group of children;
some may be lively, into everything and very friendly, while
others can be shy and prefer to keep to themselves. So use
the following details with caution; they are only meant as a
guide.

Lively minds

The most noticeable feature of clever children is the
liveliness of their minds, which comes across in many
ways, most especially in their delight with words. They're
very 'talkative' little babies, but their babbling and cooing
soon give way to a stream of toddler conversation which can
become quite serious, even by the age of three. Many of
them are reading by four years old, and then they seem to
devour every word in sight. Clever children can have effective
memories, outstandingly better than other children of the
same age, even in babyhood, and certainly by the time
they're going into their third year. A four year old, for
example, might remember going on a picnic a year before.
Parents of clever children often remark on their toddler's
amazing memories. If they're interested in something, they
can also concentrate for hours when very small.

Many clever children seem to be born with a keen edge of competitive spirit. They may compete against themselves, always trying to do better next time, or they may compete against other children in the sense of (as the song says) 'Anything you can do, I can do better'. Does your toddler try to succeed over and over gain, showing great perseverance until she does?

Even as toddlers, clever children are usually very quick to spot tiny differences and catch on to unusual associations between ideas. But toddlers still don't know very much about the world they live in, as the following conversation shows:

Toddler You can't build houses on hills.
Mother Yes you can, look at the houses going up that hill.
Toddler But how can the floors be flat then?
Mother Well, you either have to dig the house into the hill or let it stick out like a balcony.
Toddler (trying to keep her end up in the conversation) I think you should build houses 'properly', even if the floors would be slanting. You know, just put them on the hill. People could go up and down inside. It would save a lot of trouble.

Awareness

Some clever toddlers can use their very high levels of awareness to take in information very quickly, sometimes catching your meaning before you reach the end of your sentence. Sometimes they seem to be able to take information in from more than one source at a time, such as listening to two conversations and getting full measure from both. There are adults who feel that they can do this too, but their way of going about it is different – they switch attention and memory, putting a little of what they've heard into store, then returning to it when they've heard the next bit. They jump back and forth mentally to keep the two inputs open, but are actually only paying attention to one at a time. There may be times when you're surprised to find that your toddler has heard every word of your conversation, and that he can also repeat exactly what he heard on the radio at the same time.

Their heightened awareness often allows clever toddlers to imagine what it's like to be another person. This means that they're exceptionally good at copying other people's behaviour and learning fast from the experience. Unfortunately this can give them the appearance of being quite grown-up, and is easily mistaken for the genuine maturity that they will grow into later.

It often happens that clever children are also highly sensitive. It is this sensitivity that allows the child to be so bright in the first place, because it enables him to absorb a wide variety of information and ideas that less able children might miss. But sometimes that extra sensitivity may make it hard for him to bear even normal criticism, so that he may take it too much to heart and seem to over-react. Clever toddlers are responsive enough to gentle guidance rather than punishment, and they need praise at least as much as any other children.

Ability to learn
By ten months or so a clever baby may be quite sociable, in an almost adult way. She may be able to get hold of your attention and keep it when she wants it. A clever one year old, for example, may have learned that she's more likely to get her own way by smiling than by screaming for attention. So she may play with her half-learned new words with a smile for your delight, seeming to know that it will make you want to stay and enjoy her success.

Clever children seem to have a particularly keen appetite for learning so that, when they're given the opportunity, they grab it. As they get older their knowledge often becomes wider and deeper than that of other children, so that, for example, a six year old may have the knowledge of a nine year old. It's not that he's getting more clever all the time; it just looks that way, because he knows more. Parents may well wonder where clever children get all their knowledge from; they seem to absorb it from everywhere – television, books, people's conversations.

I was giving an intelligence test to Millicent a couple of years ago. As she was only five, I hadn't bothered to conceal the test manual, as you're supposed to. She was obviously doing very well, notably when it came to the point where she had to repeat a row of numbers backwards. 'I think I should tell you,' she piped, 'that I can read upside down.'

Independence

Clever toddlers have a sureness about what they do. They are often comfortable with themselves and take pride in their accomplishments. Sometimes they even try to dominate their parents, mischievously thinking of ways to play tricks and have fun, such as hiding Daddy's shoes when he's about to go out. Or they may want to outshine their parents, to go one better. Once I was making an arrangement over the 'phone to meet someone: 'How about Saturday afternoon?' I asked. 'I'm free.' To which my clever toddler responded proudly 'I'm free and a half!'

Even in their first few days at school, clever children are usually outstandingly independent and competent in their lessons. Some develop special interests, which they want to follow up in depth, even while they are only at nursery school. By the time they reach proper school they're really beginning to know their way around the subject. William, for example, loved classical music, and had some records which he could play as he wanted; he was very careful with them. But his reading, aged four, was still a bit wobbly on such names as Prokofiev and Tchaikovsky, so he remembered numbers for the pieces instead. One day, while out shopping with his mother, he heard something he recognised over the supermarket loudspeaker. 'Oh listen!' he cried in rapture, 'it's number 10.'

Do they need special attention?

It's not always pure pleasure to realise that you may be the parent of a very clever or even a gifted child. There are a few worrying ideas about such exceptional children, and these ideas pop up in newspapers and conversations from time to time. I've put together some answers here to questions that parents often ask me about their clever children.

Given the chance, clever children will learn faster and perform better than the average child, so it may appear as though they can do without special attention. But whether this is really so depends partly on your view of education. You may think every child should have the same education and that specially bright children will get on well enough on their own, so that most attention should go to those who need help in keeping up. But if you think every child should be educated to his full potential, then bright children will also need some special attention in order to achieve theirs. (The educational needs of exceptionally bright children are described in more detail in Chapter 9.)

I believe that all children, including the clever ones, have a right to find their education interesting and challenging. They shouldn't be bound by such learning restrictions as keeping to the average class pace all the time, so they will need some special opportunities to suit their extra ability to learn. If, in his most formative years, a clever child is wasting much of his energy in unnecessary activity, such as learning simple stages of maths when his mind is capable of jumping some of them, he can be put off the subject by the sheer drudgery of it.

The key to this is using a flexible approach. Before education became obligatory for all children, the lucky ones were educated by tutors, or in small groups. As well as receiving his father's help, Mozart, for example, had personal tutors from a very early age. He would be unlikely to have had the time he needed to develop his talent for musical competition today, in the cut and thrust of a big school. Still, you never know; Benjamin Britten's aunt, who brought him up, was very down to earth. She used to make him stop composing when bedtime came. 'If it's any good', she would say, 'it'll wait till morning.'

Should we tell the school?
Parents are often worried about seeming 'pushy' if they tell the teacher what they feel about their child's high ability.

However they do have a responsibility to their child to be honest with her teacher; if the teacher and the parents aren't working along the same lines, it is the child who is the loser. The chances are very good that the school will do its best to cooperate with parents if, rather than just appearing to claim special attention for their child, they show a genuine concern to work along with the teacher.

It's helpful to the school (and themselves) if parents write down some evidence of the child's cleverness, to take with them to the school. This could include details of pre-school reading, early talking, unusual words or ideas, musical talent and so on. It also helps if you can bring examples of the child's work along with you.

How will they cope with life?

As they get older, especially bright children usually broaden their interests more and more. This means that as well as being better than other children at school subjects, they may also have a much wider range of interests outside school. Those who are particularly interested in music, for example, will gladly spend time taking part in orchestra and choir rehearsals. Many such children seem to be good at everything, from maths to art, from sport to philosophy. Though it's hard for parents to cope with such a wide range of excellence, it's very exciting too.

Parents may worry that their children are trying too many things – over-extending and thereby exhausting themselves. But if a child is choosing his activities freely, rather than being pushed into them by an adult, there's little danger of that happening. What may seem like work to an adult may be fun to a child. Some clever children, though, settle for one thing at a time, learning everything they can about it until they're satisfied, and then dropping it, often to their parent's amazement. Our eldest son, for instance, worked intensely through jigsaw puzzles, puppet plays and steam trains, before he got on to designing pipe organs, went on to study the trombone at music college, and is now studying for a PhD in computer science at Cambridge.

Clever children can be quite bossy in group games, since they often feel they remember and understand the rules better than others. This behaviour doesn't make them popular, and they may need a little gentle guidance on being tactful. Alternatively, to avoid the problem, they may turn to athletics or non-competitive sports. It sometimes happens that clever children are among the youngest in their class, because they've been advanced a year, or because they started school a year early. Teachers and classmates easily forget that they are so young, when they appear to be just small. This is a particular problem for boys in secondary schools. Remind yourself and your child that if he appears to be undersized, it's really because he's a whole year younger than the others. It can still be hard for a child to live with this, though, and my long term follow-up research has shown that moving up a class or more isn't always worth it.

Does cleverness in children last?

The question of 'Early ripe – early rot' is often asked about children who are advanced for their years. To some people it seems positively unhealthy to be clever in childhood; as Shakespeare wrote in *Richard III*, 'So wise so young, they say, do never live long.' But that idea is quite untrue today. For every Chopin, Shelley or Brontë who died before their time, there are many more Menuhins, Ted Hughes, Doris Lessings or Somerset Maughams who have lived to a ripe old age. The famous precocious children who died young were born into an age when medicine was less effective, and their less clever and less famous contemporaries also risked exactly the same fate of a premature death.

On the whole, especially clever children do turn out to be pretty bright adults. However, some might be unusually advanced at the time they are noticed and subsequently return to a more average level as they grow up. It's a bit like height; a girl may stand head and shoulders above the others of her age until she reaches adolescence, and then might stop growing. As the others continue to grow, they catch up with her, and perhaps even pass her. It's impossible for parents to judge whether their child will always be ahead of others, either in height or in mental ability. All you can do is fit her up as comfortably as you can at the time, both in her clothes and her education.

What about really gifted children?

This book is concerned with a much wider range of children than those who could be described as gifted. But it does also cover gifted children, who have just as much right to an appropriate education as any other group. They do, however, have some special needs and vulnerabilities.

The gifted are the brightest children of all – the top 2 per cent of children on any measure; those whose abilities make them quite outstanding, head and shoulders above all others of the same age. This is not to say that their giftedness is always obvious, no matter what their potential might be. All children can run into problems which prevent them from doing their best. It can happen, for example, that gifted children do not get the right learning materials – you can't speak a foreign language if you have never heard it. Just like any other child, the gifted can have emotional problems, and these are rarely anything to do with their abilities. There may be trouble at home, for instance, which can use up the energy they might have put towards developing their gifts. Emotional trouble can get in the way of learning.

Parents usually have a good idea of their children's abilities, as I found in the course of my research. But parents (at least in Great Britain) hesitate to use the word 'gifted', perhaps because it sounds like boasting. However it is really just a description, an adjective, which indicates that the child has some ability which is at a distinctly higher level than other children's.

Children may be gifted all round, or in just one specific area. Indeed, some are remarkably good at almost everything, whereas others may have just a special aptitude for certain subjects, such as fine art or mathematics. But whatever they have the potential to do, gifted children still need plenty of the right kind of help in order to develop their talents. They need expert tuition and provision; without it, gifted children cannot make the most of their gifts, and they do not automatically, as is often said, rise like cream to the top. If one is to make the cream rise to the top of a cup of coffee, the mixture must be prepared correctly and the cream put on in the right way, dripped off a warm spoon.

Whatever their gifts, however deep and mature their level of thinking, gifted children are normally happy and healthy. You couldn't pick one out in a crowd, because they don't look different from any others. I have often had the impression, though, that they have a more penetrating way of looking at you.

3
YOUR AMAZING BABY

It is only relatively recently – since the 1960s – that psychologists have taken a concerned interest in newborn babies, and begun to make scientific observations of their behaviour. For centuries it had been thought that at birth a baby was just, in the philosopher John Locke's words, a *tabula rasa*, a clean slate, on which parents had merely to 'write' correctly in order to bring up a perfect child. In contrast, the French philosopher Jean-Jacques Rousseau believed that a child was born wise, a 'noble savage', and if left to develop naturally would become a moral and knowledgeable adult.

From the newborn's own point of view the world was, according to the 19th-century psychologist William James, just 'a blooming buzzing confusion'. On that basis, parents were advised to guard their babies from disturbances such as bright lights or spicy foods, since these would only add to their confusion. Be warned that some of this feeling that the baby must be kept unstimulated at all times still persists – a situation which produces bored babies.

Later, in this century, babies' daily lives became so rigidly ordered that even the newborn had to be taught to 'behave' – to be hungry on command (four-hourly) and to cry at appropriate times (just before feeding time). This scheduling was ordained by the New Zealand doctor, Truby King, who caused enormous guilt in those parents who dared to pick their babies up in between permitted times. This was followed by Dr John Bowlby's dictum, which caused at least as much distress, that babies should never be without mother (fathers were exempt in those days). But Dr Benjamin Spock loosened the reins in the 1950s, and was consequently blamed for the swinging sixties generation of young people. He changed his mind in his later years. Fortunately, such baby gurus are much less powerful nowadays, possibly because we are paying more attention to the babies themselves.

Watching tiny babies and seeing how they react to gentle experiments, such as choosing which flavour they like best, is slow and expensive work. But by patient study, psychologists have now accumulated enough evidence to show clearly that newborns are neither blank sheets nor to be disciplined like army recruits. Instead, they come ready supplied with a whole set of personal characteristics and, most excitingly, a will to find things out. How they progress in their early discoveries, though, is very dependent on the attitudes, understanding and knowledge of those who look after them. As this is usually (but not always) the mother, I shall refer to her as the baby's earliest care-giver.

WHERE BRIGHTNESS BEGINS

The making of a bright child can be said to begin even before conception. Although there's not much that prospective parents can do about their ancestry and the genetic characteristics they are passing on, they can be effective in giving a good start to the next generation.

Perhaps the single most important event in a child's life is her parents' decision to have a baby. A truly wanted baby has the advantage of starting life with positive feelings from both parents about bringing up children. Wanted babies are usually easier to bring up, and have less colic, than unexpected ones; furthermore, positive welcoming feelings are not always around when the conception is a 'mistake'. Not very long ago, before the pill and other reliable forms of contraception were widely available, there was always the risk that making love would result in a another human being coming to live on the earth for more than half a century. Now, for most of us, there is a good chance that future generations will be wanted and prepared for, well before they're born.

Any woman's health and habits can, of course, have undesirable side effects on her unborn child. Cigarette smoke, whether from the mother's own cigarettes or from a smoky atmosphere, has been found to lower the newborn's birth-weight. This in turn can lower his resistance to illness, so that he does not thrive as he should. Children whose mothers smoke heavily (20–30 cigarettes a day) when pregnant are found to have more difficulties at school, and are more likely to be over-active. Alcohol, too, even as little as an ounce a day, can be harmful for the unborn baby. Pregnant women who drink heavily are found to have low birth-weight babies, who are less well coordinated in their movements, sluggish and hard to arouse. The conclusion is simple, and the evidence is there: cut out the poisonous drugs of nicotine and alcohol, at least while you are pregnant.

Good food and exercise are greatly beneficial to mothers-to-be and their babies. But it is only when the diet is abysmal, such as in times of famine or prolonged poverty, that the baby's abilities are likely to be permanently affected by lack of nourishment before birth. Older women (over 35 years) do face a somewhat increased risk of having a backward child, though this risk is decreased if the father is younger. Good antenatal care is usually freely available in developed countries, and risks are enormously reduced for those who take advantage of it.

The best possible birth

A much more difficult problem for parents is how to ensure that the baby is born as perfectly as it has developed in the womb. The quality of maternity services varies from country to country and from district to district. It is possible to find out what kind of provision is available in different areas, and you may possibly be able to arrange to have your baby in an area or hospital with the best newborn health records. At the very worst, this could make a difference between life and death, or between a spastic or a normal life for the baby – these may depend on having the facilities available to take swift action, where necessary, to prevent even the slightest damage at birth to baby or mother.

Sometimes, as a result of deep psychological probing or under hypnosis, people say they remember what it felt like before they were born. They mostly tell of the cosiness of the womb, and describe how terrible it was when they were struggling and being pushed out. Although these may well be true, they may also come from imagination or half-memories of what adults know of births. However, some of these stories are found across the world, in many cultures.

In fact it is biologically possible for the baby to have an inkling of awareness during the final weeks in the womb. Soon before their birth babies have been seen to make simple movements in reaction to noise or touch, movements that they will make in a more complex way after they are born. Examples are the beginnings of hand grasping and turning the face towards a touch. It's possible that even a month before birth a baby can learn to adapt to circumstances such as noise or very bright light, but this capacity is not seriously tested until after birth.

Based on these observations, there has been some concern recently to treat babies with great delicacy at birth. The French doctor Frederick Leboyer advises that the baby be born in silence, in a dimly lit room, then placed on her mother's tummy, with the cord uncut, and gently stroked, while each gets used to the other. The idea is to provide as smooth an introduction as possible for a birth-shocked individual into the rough world she is to inhabit. We do not know, though, whether this method of birth has any effect on the child's future emotional or intellectual development – research results so far are inconclusive.

This style of birthing assumes great awareness by the baby of what's happening to him. But, biologically, nature has a way of cutting off consciousness at times when things get too much to bear. For example, newborn babies simply drop into sleep when conditions are too stimulating; furthermore, most babies suffer from some shortage of oxygen during birth, which further lowers their awareness. What is more, the brain rhythms which would be needed for a true appreciation of what's happening aren't yet developed in the newborn, but develop slowly as the brain grows. Their absence provides a built-in protection against the possibility of more mental stimulation than the baby can take. But a quiet gentle time of birth does at least provide the mother with a pleasant experience, which can help her to get to know her new baby more easily.

The time immediately after birth is undoubtedly very important for mothers in developing positive feelings about their babies. Some hospitals, though, still separate mothers from their newborn babies, only allowing them to come together for feeding and changing. Mothers who are separated in this way sometimes find they are less confident about handling and mothering the baby than those who've had their babies close by from the beginning. Psychologists working on mother–newborn relationships have found not only that, at the time of birth, mothers

develop a 'readiness' – a sort of maternal sensitivity – to
become attached to their babies, but that this readiness
needs immediate close physical contact in order to be
effective.

It is very important for mothers and their babies to be
together from the time of delivery; the first three days seem
to be especially important. And fathers too seem to be
specially sensitive at their baby's birth. Those who see their
babies being born feel closer to them and hold them more
intimately. This also applies to those who miss the birth,
but see their babies immediately afterwards.

New parents should ask for the mother and baby to be
allowed to stay together. Although the hospital staff may
say that babies disturb other new mothers on the ward,
every mother and baby has the same need, and it's
psychologically healthier for all of them to be together. It
may be said that babies are kept away from mothers to
reduce the risk of infection, but it sometimes seems to be
more a case of administrative tidiness. If the hospital won't
agree, then the simplest answer is probably for the mother
to go home as soon as she can.

Sometimes, painkilling drugs given to a mother during
labour can make both the mother and the baby drowsy and
so less responsive after birth. This very early dulling of
sensitivity may possibly have longer-term consequences
because of its effects on the newly developing
mother–newborn relationship. Measurements taken of
mother–baby behaviour during the first year of life have
shown that mothers who were affected by drugs given at
the time of birth have to work harder to form a good
relationship than those who were not. Obviously drugs have
to be used at times, but they do sometimes have
side-effects, so play safe and avoid them if you can. They
are used in some places more than others and mothers can
refuse them if they wish.

What you can do before and during the birth

- Try to stay calm during pregnancy.
- Avoid harmful drugs such as nicotine and alcohol.
- Take care of yourself; attend for regular antenatal care.
- Avoid drugs during delivery if you can.
- If possible, ask for a peaceful atmosphere during the baby's birth.
- Try to keep in close contact with your baby from birth, in order to get to know each other better.
- If loving feelings for the baby aren't there from the start, then work towards them with as much patience as you can manage. Tell someone at the hospital or clinic about the way you feel.
- Talk freely with your partner about feelings for each other and for the baby; for her own emotional security, a baby needs her parents to know exactly where they stand.

Welcoming the newcomer

Like many relationships, that of parent with child is undoubtedly influenced by the parents' first impressions of the child (we really don't know about the baby's first impressions of her parents). Most parents are intensely keen to see their new baby look at them, and they will try to stimulate her by stroking her face – it's part of the process of getting to know one another. Although most people assume that mothers will love their newborn babies on sight, it doesn't always happen. Love and acceptance don't appear on demand, and the baby's physical appearance and behaviour may be partly responsible for this. Certainly, some babies are easier to love than others – mothering a tiny version of your least favourite relative may not be easy.

Naturally enough, parents have expectations and fears for their unborn child – and also for themselves – before the birth. They may find themselves disappointed or even angry when the baby arrives, but it isn't always acceptable to admit to these feelings, either to themselves or to anyone else. However, if you can admit to bad feelings, it usually makes them easier to cope with. For their part, babies can sense parental tension, and they react to it by crying. In this way, a particular kind of tense family lifestyle may be set up, unknowingly, right from the beginning. Even by the time they leave hospital, the mother and baby relationship can be partly moulded, so that what goes on in the hospital is very important indeed.

However in nearly every case, any initial lack of feeling for a baby will be overcome sooner or later. Handle the baby as lovingly as possible, talk to him, give him all your attention, and slowly but surely you can expect truly loving feelings to come. With them will grow an understanding and sensitivity which are the roots of his own feelings of well-being.

The most important part of a new baby's mental development is his social life. Obviously, physical well-being is very important indeed for a baby's survival, but all the handling, powdering and feeding that go on every day have a remarkable psychological spin-off, in that they develop the parents' relationship with the baby. Parents can use this to help their baby develop into a competent child.

A mother is a baby's first courier, the link between the newcomer and the outside world. It's a parent's job to help the baby take his place in society, and this responsibility starts from the moment of birth. That is when intellectual life begins, and neither parent nor baby can remain unaffected by the way it progresses.

Though no one can read a baby's mind, we can watch how she behaves with other people. It's from there that we can work out how her mental life is progressing. Here are just some of the mental facilities a brand new baby has.

- *Seeing* A newborn can focus both eyes on a point about 20 centimetres away, follow a moving object with her eyes and, certainly within two weeks, distinguish colours.

- *Hearing* A newborn can tell the differences in loudness and pitch of sound in voices, and distinguish some similar sounds like 'pah' and 'bah'. She can be soothed by rhythmic sounds.
- *Smelling* This sense is well developed at birth, and newborns have strong likes (milk) and dislikes (ammonia and liquorice).
- *Tasting* A newborn prefers sweet to salty tastes and can tell the difference between sour and bitter.
- *Touch* Newborns are responsive to touch all over their bodies, girls possibly more so than boys.
- *Vocalising* The first sound a baby makes is its birth-cry, which is simply a reflex inhalation of air, soon to be followed by distinct cries of hunger or distress.

Conversations

Although newborn babies can't speak, they're great little communicators. From the beginning, mothers and babies are sensitive to each other's messages and start to have two-way 'conversations'. At first the signals aren't very easy to detect, which is probably why they stayed unrecognised for so long. Mothers have undoubtedly always been aware of it, but perhaps no one thought to ask them about it.

Sometimes the baby will try something out and the mother has to adjust, and sometimes it's the other way round. The 'conversations' often run in cycles. One such might begin with a baby looking at his mother. She responds by looking at him, and touching and talking to him. He watches and smiles back ... then he begins to turn away ... she tries to keep his interest ... he closes his eyes. That is the end of that cycle. Either one of them may re-start it, and the process may take place many times without a break.

These exchanges, which take place over the first two or three months of life, indicate the style of relationship which the mother–baby couple will use together for the rest of their lives. Since each one of them is affected by messages from the other and reacts to these, each controls the other to some extent. Mothers who realise and accept that the baby has an active part to play, right from the beginning, will treat their baby as a person and give her the best possible start in life. This new person has her own needs, wants and intentions, which her mother learns to recognise and translate into words for her: 'So you want a cuddle, do you?' or 'Now, you're nice and cosy and ready for sleep.'

Mother–baby 'conversations' are not quite democratic, though. Mother usually takes the lead in suggesting and demanding certain behaviour from the baby. She does this by making approving noises, telling him when she is pleased, and trying to discourage behaviour which she thinks is unacceptable. A sensitive mother knows when the baby is receiving her loud and clear; it's not just his behaviour that she's affecting, but his whole way of learning. It's because the mother sees her baby as a growing person that he comes, over time, to behave in something like the approved way.

Although the father's feelings about his baby aren't quite as physical – he didn't get pregnant or give birth – he normally feels very strongly attached to his baby. Unfortunately, though, the average amount of time that fathers in western culture spend alone with their babies of under a year old is usually less than half an hour a day. Yet playing and 'talking' with her father also helps the baby's mind to develop, and is very important for a balanced outlook.

The success of the communication between mothers and babies depends very much on the sensitivity and tolerance of both parties, mother and baby. That's why it's so difficult to judge the specific effects of a particular style of mothering. The individual nature of each baby affects his relationships and his parents' behaviour almost as powerfully as his parents affect him. No two babies respond to influences and experiences in exactly the same way, so that different styles of caring can have different effects on different babies. Parents are certainly not completely responsible for their baby's psychological world.

How babies organise parents

The deep love that grows between a baby and her mother
starts at birth, though it often takes months to develop
fully. Babies take a very active part in developing this love;
it isn't just a one-way process. The baby's part in forging
the link takes the form of crying, smiling, making noises –
anything that will keep her mother close. The baby will
claim more attention for herself when she's hungry, in pain,
tired or ill than when she's well fed and comfortable. But
babies vary in the way they approach this task.

Some babies are not very good at giving positive
feedback; they don't give their mothers much reassurance.
For example, the baby may not appear to be delighted

What you can do for tiny babies

- You can't spoil a newborn baby, so feel free to try;
  you can only do good by giving him lots of
  cuddling and attention.
- Keep it very simple at this early stage and don't
  spend money on toys which won't interest him yet.
  Two or three items at a time will do.
- Let him see different things going on by moving
  him around the house with you and propping him
  up so that he can watch the world comfortably.
- From time to time hang a sparkling mobile
  securely over his cot, for him to look at. Put it
  about 20 centimetres from his face, so that he can
  focus on it.
- Paint a big face on cardboard and hang it where he
  can see it. Babies like faces and he will turn to look
  at it when he feels like it.
- Put the baby on his tummy for at least half an
  hour a day and for five to ten minutes after meals,
  to strengthen his neck muscles. If he can move his
  head easily, he'll see more. But watch to see that he
  is breathing properly.
- Keep him with you as much as possible.

when he sees his mother, yet he may show his feelings when she goes out of sight by crying. On the other hand, some do the opposite. A mother should watch out for the different ways that her baby uses to hold her attention, and should let him know by an extra cuddle that his efforts are being successful; this increases his sense of well-being and security.

But there are also babies who don't seem at all sure of what they want, so they try out a variety of approaches to see which is the most satisfying. This can be bewildering for the parents, who are doing their best to make their baby happy. Have patience and go along with your baby's attempts to communicate, maybe even for a couple of months. Together, you'll soon work out a system that is reasonably satisfactory for the whole family.

Babies in Western culture are usually fed on demand, which effectively means that they are taking the initiative in calling for food. A nursing mother may respond to her baby's cry by the oozing of a little milk from her breasts. But in South America, for example, the Mayan Indian mother starts producing milk when her baby merely moves. The Mayan mother expects to feed her baby before he gets hungry enough to cry; she feels for him and anticipates his wishes, rather than waiting for him to ask. Thus, even from the time of birth, we in the West place a hefty burden of responsibility on those tiny shoulders. Western babies are expected to make many of their own decisions about their lives; adults then respond to these, according to the way they interpret the scarcely practised instructions.

Another example of this is the way the Western baby takes a hand in organising his own comfort. He shows how he would prefer to be held by complaining if it's not right and he feels uncomfortable. His mother soon gets to know his sources of comfort, as he himself learns what they are, and communication between the couple improves. By contrast, the Mayan baby has no choice, being firmly wrapped in a traditional carrying sling.

Not only does a Western baby have to demand his food

and sort out his comfort; he also has to organise his sleep pattern to his own best advantage – although some babies don't seem to be very good at it. Time spent with adults is important to a baby, at the very least for food and comfort, so he has to try to be awake when people are around and asleep when they're not. From the newborn's point of view, he can't be sure that there will always be someone around, and he soon learns that he's unlikely to be fed or comforted until he demands it.

Not surprisingly, the baby may suffer an unfortunate side-effect from all this organising activity, and that is anxiety. If you're not sure where your next meal's coming from, right from the start, some feeling of insecurity is not unreasonable.

Some of this anxiety or insecurity can be seen in older children, and arises from the differences between the way boys and girls are brought up. Girl babies are often allowed to be more dependent than boys; for example, their crying times may be shorter before they're seen to, and they're cuddled more than boys without having to ask for it first. What happens then is that the older boys get, the less easy they find it to ask for help from others; they are supposed to be more independent than girls. This can be seen also in

---

What you can do to coordinate with your baby

- Watch out for any signs she gives you, such as a glance, a cry or a hand movement, and react to them promptly to show you've got the message.
- Try to keep in tune with your baby. If you know what's on her mind, you can think ahead of her and anticipate her wishes. That way she can relax in the confidence that she will be provided for.
- Make sure that babies get lots of loving contact; in particular, give a boy as much as you would to a girl.
- Be kind, as well as loving, to your baby.

grown men, who have a greater fear of dependency than women do.

Often, unknowingly, parents encourage signs of independence in babies of both sexes from the time they are born. Little signs of independence are usually watched for, and approved of warmly – like a baby pushing away the bottle when she's had enough. I once heard a mother, speaking for her baby's independence, say 'We had to leave the maternity ward early as Roger [the baby] wanted to go home.'

The more freedom we give our babies to organise their own lives, the more kindness and security they need. Love and kindness are not the same thing, and babies need kindness too.

Can you tell if a newborn baby is bright?

Clever babies are probably more alert when they're born than other babies. Some can hold their heads up alone for a moment or two, right from the start, and seem to be looking around and taking life in with great interest. Sometimes doctors and nurses will tell parents if a baby seems to be more alert than usual, but then they may say that to all new parents.

A baby who is particularly sensitive and responsive is often very bright. You can feel this responsiveness when you hold her. For example, if she seems to back away from something, it shows that she can distinguish between what's pleasant for her and what's not – and that's the beginning of mental activity. More sensitive babies are also more easily tickled.

The earlier you see your baby smile, the more likely she is to be bright. Though this isn't a totally reliable sign, it is an indication, and very early smilers often turn out to be bright, lively children.

Very intelligent children are often bigger and heavier at birth, though not always. The reason for this is that big healthy babies are more likely to be born to mothers who have been well nourished and cared for in their pregnancies. It's those same mothers who are more likely to give their children the best educational help at home, which will show up later in intelligence tests. It's possible, too, that heavier babies have a psychological advantage as well as a better physical start in life, because they have reason to be more contented than other babies. They can take in more food each time, for example, so that they need less frequent feeding and can turn their energies in more intellectual directions. In addition, their parents, relieved of the constant preoccupation with feeding and cleaning that smaller babies need, may feel that such a baby is more of a social person and so behave differently towards him. So even from birth, heavier and more attractive babies probably find themselves in a more pleasant and emotionally supportive world than lighter ones, and will benefit from this initial good fortune in many ways.

Different abilities in newborns develop at different rates and, though there's some coordination between them, it would never do to measure the growth of one or two abilities and judge the rest on that basis. Some of a baby's skills are related to her degree of physical development, others to experience, and some to both. In trying to judge very early signs of cleverness, always look at your baby as a whole person. In general, you could say that very bright babies show all-round advancement in their development, and the likelihood is that, with their parents' help, they will keep that advantage.

WHAT A BRIGHT BABY NEEDS

The most important psychological benefit that parents can give their new baby is super-generous amounts of loving physical cuddling. This means holding the baby in an upright position a lot, and having plenty of eye contact. It gives the baby the reassurance he needs to build up his feeling of security, which in turn builds the base for exploration and learning, and later for self-reliance. You can't 'spoil' tiny babies by cuddling them too much.

Research on newborn babies in Zambia by the American Professor Brazelton found that by the time they were five days old they were already more advanced than American babies, and even more so by ten days old. They kept up this lead until they were about two years old, when the American babies he studied began to overtake them on simple tests of mental ability. He thought that this very early advance was due to the way the babies were handled. The Zambian tribal mother carries her baby around in a cloth sling, usually on her back. The baby is fed when he cries, sleeps with his mother, and is handled quite roughly by Western standards; for example, a Zambian mother positions the baby on her back by gripping one of his elbows under her armpit and swinging him over her shoulder. The later slowing up of his progress is probably due to the arrival of another baby, when he is usually pushed aside, loses his supply of mother's milk, and goes on to a nutritionally poor diet.

It's the close physical contact between mothers and babies that makes it very much easier for them to get to know one another. When the mother is holding the baby close and looking at him, she's in a much better position to make immediate responses to his signals. The quicker her response, the more likely the baby is to retain his new learning. Babies aren't much good at remembering what's gone before (see pages 9–10), so a mother may have to respond to the same signals over and over again, and this is easier for them both if she's close by at the right times.

Babies have a real need to build up a close relationship from the beginning. They seem to be satisfied with one good one, though they can cope with several. They need the opportunity to explore their world within their relationships, most particularly by means of their 'conversations' with others. This is where the foundations of understanding and language are laid. The baby's activities are not simply directed towards making life more comfortable, though they are a positive attempt to make his life more lively – in a sense, to stir things up, so he can learn from his own sensitivities and vulnerabilities.

Babies are born predisposed to social life, which enables them, in time, to develop into social people. The newborn human baby needs love (physical and emotional), adult responsiveness, stimulation and total acceptance.

ISN'T SHE A BRIGHT ONE!

The human mind is active right from the start. Soon after birth, a baby begins to select and organise her experiences. All the time, when she's awake, a tiny baby is reacting to what's going on around her and doing her best to cope with the information she takes in. Sights and sounds don't just flow over her in a haphazard way, they are attended to; some are dismissed, and some are assigned to the beginnings of memory. Right from the start the baby is striving to learn, trying out different ways of doing things, experimenting all the time and judging the value of the results. Although she is barely aware (in the adult sense) of what she is doing, the world is a very complicated business to sort out, and she gets on with it right away.

Mental development is not something that parents can impose from the outside, nor is it merely a matter of sitting back and allowing natural abilities to unfold like a flower bud. It's an interactive process, in which the baby has a big part of his own to play. A baby searches out his own learning, and never depends entirely on what chance may bring for his mental stimulation – he makes things happen by cooing or crying to attract attention. If a baby were only to lie back passively and wait for experience, very little might happen; he certainly wouldn't be able to practise communication, which he so clearly does do, at the start of life.

When a baby is born she has some unthinking physical reflexes, and these should not be confused with mental activity. She can, for example, grasp an adult finger if it's forced into her little fist. If she's held in the right position, she can make walking movements; and when laid flat on her face, she can raise her head. But though these reflexes are useful, the newborn hasn't any actual skills; they still have to be learnt.

Video recordings have provided a big breakthrough in

understanding very tiny babies. Babies' behaviour is often
so fleeting that much of what we can now see in close-up
and in slow motion could never have been seen before. The
video tapes can be run through over and over again, until
every detail of the scene is familiar to the viewer;
sometimes subtle movements may only be spotted after
several replays.

A double-screen technique has been devised that splits
the pictures of a mother with her baby so they can be
shown on two separate screens at the same time. This
method provides a view of the behaviour of each when they
are together, which is easier for comparison than having
them in the same frame. Because it's only in the last few
years that these techniques have been used, even fairly
recent textbooks on child development haven't been able to
report the findings, and many details are still to be found
only in research documents. Here are just some of the
discoveries.

Eye contact
The baby's inborn capacity for eye-to-eye contact provides
the key factor in forging the link between mother and baby.
From birth, babies seem to be fascinated by the human
face, and can recognise their mother's face within a week.
By one month old a baby can take in enough information
about faces to sort out familiar from unfamiliar ones. All
newborn babies are short-sighted, but mothers usually hold
their faces naturally at the the right distance from their
baby's – about 20 centimetres (8 inches) away.

Watching
From birth, a baby can follow a large object with his eyes
for a few seconds, providing it's held at the right distance,
though he can't manage smaller ones yet. Within a week,
he'll move his eyes purposefully about and will soon
become selective in what he looks at, such as following his
own hand movements. Just a few days after birth, almost
all babies can follow a red light, moving their heads and
eyes to do this. During this action they focus all their

behaviour on the task of coordinating vision, body movement and attention.

Listening

Within seconds of birth, babies can detect the direction of a sound and turn their face towards it. At only 12 hours old they can spot the difference between human speech and other sounds, reacting with barely visible rhythmic movements which show up on a slow-motion video recording. Mother and baby learn about each other by using sound, 'talking' and 'listening' to each other.

A baby shouldn't be left alone for long periods of time with no one around to talk or listen to. This is because she needs to be able to practise the constant wordless 'chatter' with other people that forms this very early foundation of her future language.

Sensitivity

Babies are born with all five senses working. Although no two babies are alike in their alertness and in the speed of their responses, all are very sensitive to changes in what's going on around them. A newborn will startle or cry at what seems like only a barely noticeable change in the surroundings, such as a new voice speaking. A baby will also close his eyes or turn his head away from a light that's too bright or a movement that is too disturbing for him.

Parents should watch out to see that their baby is not overloaded with messages. Otherwise, one may learn just to 'switch off', using shorter and shorter spans of attention and missing out on aspects of this very early learning. The parents' sensitivity must be the guide; keep looking at your baby to see whether she turns away from your attentions. If she does, then cut down for a while on trying to make her react.

Smiling

Mothers have said that their babies could smile by the end of the second week, to which doctors and nurses have invariably replied that it's only wind. Now, thanks to video, we have much evidence to show that mothers are often right. These very early smiles are in fact the products of highly organised behaviour, which shows the beginning of thought.

These early smiles are different from later smiles, though, as they arise from feelings that the baby has inside, rather than as responses to other peoples' smiles. The first few may be a reaction to the mother's voice, or they may be due to a change in the baby's surroundings. Too great a change, though, may only produce tension and crying: too little, and the baby will ignore it. In a couple of months, as the baby gets more sophisticated, these spontaneous smiles are increasingly replaced by genuine social smiles.

Copying

The new video techniques have shown that, contrary to previous opinion, babies can imitate their mother's facial and body movements to some extent soon after birth. A 14-day-old baby can even imitate a finger movement in an adult sitting next to him.

Babies begin to imitate patterns of speech movement with their lips from a few weeks old, but they are able to distinguish between some different speech sounds even from birth. Speech begins here. Talk to your baby as much as you like; he'll understand your tone, even if the words are beyond him, and he will like the rhythm.

Crying

Crying is the main means of early voice communication that the baby uses to bring someone near her. There are a variety of cries, with different strengths and rhythms, all of which send different messages. Parents, for example, quickly get to know the difference between a cry of hunger and one of fear.

Don't let a baby 'cry it out' too often, as it restricts developing communication skills. Give regular prompt response to cries when you can, as this is more likely to bring about a better quality of relationship between you and your baby, and so eventually cut down on the crying. When the baby learns that her cries are likely to be answered immediately, she'll be more inclined to branch out and try other, more subtle, forms of getting your attention as well, and she will also be less intense in her demands.

Answering a tiny baby's cry doesn't lead to a 'spoilt' child, as is sometimes thought, though some babies are more easily soothed than others. An 'easy' baby will respond readily to a wide variety of calming efforts on the part of his parents, such as being rocked, stroked or shifted from a flat to an upright position. Some say that girl babies are more 'soothable'. A fussy baby may not respond very much to normal soothing, so that her mother may feel less adequate as a mother. In this way, a baby's 'soothability' dictates the kind of care that she receives – the more easily soothed a baby is, the more pleasant attention she gets.

The best way to stop a baby crying is to hold her up on your shoulder. This usually makes her open her eyes and look around. If your baby is one of those who aren't very cuddly, try raising up her baby-seat instead, putting it on a table for example, so that she can look around.

Whatever you do, it's a fact that some babies cry more than others, and parents have to judge for themselves how best to cope with their baby's crying. If it's getting on top of you and she doesn't seem to be responding to your attentions, don't hesitate to seek help, and don't be put off trying because you are made to feel over-fussy.

PREMATURE BIRTH

Being born before time isn't usually considered to give a baby the best start in life, though 8 per cent of babies begin that way. But some very recently discovered facts allow us to understand how the effects of prematurity and low birth-weight can be overcome.

Judging babies' mental development poses a problem. Overall, the baby's age after birth is usually the best basis for measurement, but the development of some abilities does depend on physical maturity, and this may not coordinate exactly in a premature baby. Brain waves, for example, develop in accordance with age, so a premature baby is likely to have a similar brain wave pattern and be as mentally developed as a full-term baby of the same age. On the other hand, the way the baby's vision develops is tied to his rate of physical growth, which is slower in a premature baby.

Unfortunately, premature babies often have to cope with extra disadvantages, such as more stress than other babies, in addition to their early birth. A premature baby incubator, for example, though vital for life, isn't the ideal place for encouraging mental development. In the hospital unit, light and sound usually go on 24 hours a day. This is an abnormal situation, and can affect the new baby's delicate mental and muscle coordination; being in conditions like these would have bad effects on an adult too. But the main problem for an incubator baby is the lack of normal experiences to learn from, together with the overload of disorganised, confusing experiences of sights and sounds, which can go on for weeks.

Where it's possible to offer these babies a more normal environment, it can be seen to make a big improvement in their overall development. For example, babies who have been taken from their incubators regularly for cuddling, or who lie on softer bedding, such as sheepskin, or have rhythmic sounds played to them, gain weight faster, are mentally more responsive and are better coordinated than those who do not have these experiences.

These hiccups in a premature baby's development call for extra attention when she comes home, so that she can catch up with anything she may have missed out on. For example, because the baby's vision isn't as well developed as a full-term baby's, the mother will find that she has to make a special effort to build up her relationship with her baby; eye-to-eye contact, which is so vital to intellectual development, may be more difficult if the baby is premature. It's essential for the mother to put a lot into building up this relationship. Though it won't be as much of a two-way partnership as it will be later, it is a beginning.

Because of these less rewarding visual responses, as well as the baby's limited ability to pay attention (due to immaturity), parents of a premature baby need to take special care to see that the baby gets his full share of experiences once he's home. Some researchers, though, have described a 'catch up' phenomenon built into children's development. In rural Guatemala, newborn infants are kept in a darkened room and are allowed very little stimulation during the first year of their lives, which is meant to protect them. When measured for mental development, they were found to be retarded at the ages of two to three years old, but they caught up, more or less, in later childhood. This phenomenon probably also applies to children who are hospitalised or ill-nourished for some time after birth.

All babies are physically at their most vulnerable at birth and in the first few weeks of life, which is why medical advice must normally predominate at this time. Parents whose babies are in special medical care sometimes feel that their own natural feelings about wanting to hold them should be kept under control, except at permitted times like feeding. But it's very important for the psychological growth of all babies, however physically fragile, that they should begin to make physical contact and build up relationships from birth. It may be necessary in some hospitals to insist on at least stroking your baby, and you can always talk to her, but doctors and nurses are usually ready to fit in with parents' wishes for the baby's benefit, so there may not be a problem.

In these first few weeks of life, parents' most trustworthy guide to coping is their own sensitivity to the baby's searching and exploring activities. Part of that sensitivity lies in knowing what the baby is capable of doing, and part of it is in helping her to practise her brand new learning.

What you can do for a tiny baby's developing intelligence
From birth:

- A baby is aware from the start, so encourage him to develop a taste for exploration, e.g. by holding your face and bright objects fairly close to his eyes. He can then see and touch with his fingers, so that he also learns from feeling.
- Be sensitive to what interests him, such as your hair or a strange noise, and encourage his involvement with these things.
- Put a mirror (firmly secured) over his cot, about 20 centimetres (8 inches) from his face, so that he can see his reflection. He'll have a lot of fun pulling faces at himself. Attach it to a semi-rigid structure, such as a length of plastic, for him to reach up for when he's able to.
- Don't put a great number of objects in or around the cot; too much 'enrichment' only turns him off.
- Listen to his cries and coos, and react to them promptly.
- Make a 'cradle-gym' of toys he can reach, strung across his cot or pram, so that he can knock them, watch them swing, and learn some hand-to-eye coordination. He won't be able to grasp them to start with, because that is still too difficult.

And from six months:

- Give him just a few tough toys that won't fall to pieces when bitten or thrown. They should not be too small (no less than 5 centimetres (2 inches) in diameter) or he may swallow them.
- Try a kick toy tied to the foot end of the cot, such as a large flat piece of foam rubber covered in vinyl, showing a big toy face and little body, and tied on with strong elastic; it will give hours of pleasure and leg exercise.

- Talk about what you're doing, such as putting on socks, all the time. Repeat the key words over and over.
- Give the baby free time on a blanket on the floor every day. He'll begin to crawl and explore more quickly.
- Let him handle things that work, like switching the light on, and when he succeeds, say 'light'. Babies also love a jack-in-the-box.
- When he begins to crawl, make safe areas for him to explore. Freedom to explore is very important.
- Always respond to a baby. But if it's difficult, for example if you are on the telephone, then break off and tell the child to 'wait a minute'. It's better than ignoring him.
- Play involving games like hide-and-seek.
- Use playpens or any other restraining devices like high chairs only as long as the baby looks contented in them. When he shows signs of boredom, take him out.
- Keep life lively for the baby by changing his scenery, talking to him, and interesting him in your daily activities.
- No one is more interesting to a baby than his parents. Exaggerate your own actions slightly to make them clearer, such as speaking slowly and making clear facial expressions and body movements.

4
FAMILY LIFE

Children's earliest education within the family has by far the greatest influence on their intellectual development than they're ever likely to receive again. The members of the family are the baby's first teachers, however the family is made up; and it is not only the parents who are important, but also brothers, sisters and other people. Each family is unique, a small group which acts as a filter for the information that comes to it from the society outside, and so provides the child with its own individual culture. Children who are fortunate enough to have a sound educationally positive home background are in a much better position to make good use of what their schools have to offer them; those who are short on home learning are that much more dependent on the educational system.

Take bright little Wendy, for example, who started school

without the practice in thinking and questioning that she could have had. Her parents hadn't realised that babies need a rich social life and had kept to a rather strict routine where she was expected to do as she was told. As a result, Wendy hadn't had all the practice she could have had at talking and being listened to. Although her teacher did try to help her, their earliest conversations went something like this:

> *Teacher* (looking at Wendy's painting) What a lovely picture. Tell me about it.
> *Wendy* Cat.
> *Teacher* A nice cat. Is it yours?
> *Wendy* Yes.
> *Teacher* What sort of a cat is it?
> *Wendy* (No answer.)

The teacher, finding that she's not getting very far with Wendy, is becoming concerned about the other 29 children in her class, so decides to try again later, when she has the time. She makes a little headway:

> *Teacher* You've done very well, Wendy. Would you like to take the picture home?
> *Wendy* Yes ... mmm ... please.

By five years old Wendy should have been able and well practised enough to talk freely about her ideas in choosing her cat for the subject of her painting. She should have been able to bring her past experiences to mind and tell the teacher about them, such as how the kitten came in a basket as a birthday present, or the day the cat herself had kittens. She should also have been able to talk about the future, like when they go to stay with Grandma at Christmas, and they will have to ask a neighbour to feed the cat. The conversation should have gone rather more like this:

> *Teacher* What a lovely picture. Tell me about it.
> *Wendy* This is my little cat and her name is Tiddles. Her eyes are yellow and they sort of go up at the corners.

But she's not very big.
Teacher How old is she?
Wendy Well, she's not very old really. Mummy gave her
to me in a basket for my birthday, when I was five. She's
a lot bigger now, but Mummy says she's not grown-up
yet. So, I suppose she'll get bigger. (And so on)

Another problem of Wendy's was that she didn't quite know
how to react when the teacher asked her oblique questions
such as 'Would you like to put your painting things away?'
She'd been so used to being told what to do, rather than
being given the job of making some of her own decisions,
that in her confusion she didn't know how to deal with that
kind of request. So the teacher had to rephrase it into 'Put
your things away now, Wendy'; then she knew what to do.
The teacher understood the problem, but she did not have
the classroom time to put it right. As a result this bright
child did not have a good chance really to enjoy the
intellectual life of which she was capable. A child such as
Wendy could well slip by unnoticed as an average member
of the class. Joan Tough's book *Focus on Meaning* explains
these sort of language problems, and how to overcome
them, in more detail.

If a newborn baby is to develop his potential, he has to
have both love and respect from his parents. Although love
is often taken to be all the emotional support a child needs,
respect is sometimes overlooked. But babies are human
beings and should be treated as such right from the start.
Sometimes, though, so-called respect is misused by parents
who attend to the baby's every demand so that their lives
revolve around him. For example, when a father said to me
'I'm often late for work because of Billy', I asked why. 'He
talks so much that I can't leave till he lets me', said his
father, and explained to me patiently that Billy would get
upset otherwise. Billy was well accustomed to wielding
such power by then, as he'd been ruling the family since he
was born four years ago. I couldn't help but feel that he
would have benefited from more structure in his life so that
he would know, for example, that Daddy would set off for

work each morning at a certain time, with or without Billy's permission.

The brightest children are more likely to come from homes that are reasonably financially secure. The sense of security and confidence in the parents are picked up by the child and help her towards the good feelings about herself that she needs in order to become competent. In making the fateful decision to have a child, parents who want the best for her should be clear in their own minds whether they can afford to go ahead. The costs of bringing another individual into the world, especially the first one, are very very high – even though it is obviously not all spent at once. The loss of the mother's earnings, even for a while, usually has to be taken into account. The more secure parents are, both financially and emotionally, the more free they are to concern themselves with the finer points of childcare. Parents who are worried or worn out by what they have to do to make ends meet find it much more difficult to provide the subtle but lasting benefits of easy conversation with their children, the right kinds of learning experiences, enough close contact, and a tranquil atmosphere for them to grow up in.

One of the most poignant facts to have emerged from many studies of children growing up is that those who start with the same potential are often found to develop and achieve very differently. Children from the best homes – educationally – go on steadily to outstrip those from less supportive homes. For example, a major study of 5,000 children was conducted across Britain in the 1960s by Dr J.B.W. Douglas, in order to find out how the children's home lives affected their educational success. The mothers' maternity care was taken into account, as well as the home lifestyle. The children were then tested at 8 years old, 11 years old and 15 years old. Douglas found that the most important influences on the children's school achievement were their parents' interest in them, their hopes for their children, and the kinds of lives they themselves led. Children who came from homes where parents did not concern themselves greatly with their children's education began to show this lack in their work at primary school, and this difference between the educationally supportive and non-supportive homes grew wider through secondary school. 'This effect,' Douglas wrote, 'extends to pupils of even high ability.' Long-term studies in many countries have found the same result.

CARING FOR BABY

A baby has a better chance to do well when he has both a mother and a father to look after him. Certainly, there are one-parent families where a single adult doing the work of two brings up children beautifully, but unfortunately that's not always the case. And it's certainly harder work. Even in families where the father's work leaves him little time to see his children, they and their mother can be noticeably supported by the fact that he is at least around at weekends. Equally, when parents change partners it can have a bad effect on their child's progress, especially during the upheaval of parting; for example, it shows up in school reports, with children doing less well than they should. Though no one can guarantee a perfect marriage, it's definitely unfair to bring children into a shaky one. Having a baby calls for genuine long-term commitment from both mother and father; it should never be an attempt to put a bad marriage right.

Working mothers

The question of whether or not mothers of young children should go out to work seems to result in an extra load of guilt for mothers, whatever they do. If they can choose to be full-time home-makers they may feel guilty about not pulling their weight financially, or feel themselves to be dull companions – 'I'm only a housewife'. Yet if they go out to work, they can feel they're depriving their children of a mother's vital presence at this delicate stage of their lives.

Most baby books are written on the assumption that mothers of young children are also housewives, and do almost all the childcare alone. But in fact about 40 per cent of mothers of young children in the west now have some work outside the home, and this is far greater in many parts of the world. Fathers are also playing a much more important part in bringing up their children than they used to, though everywhere there is still some way to go before parenting is equally shared.

Fortunately, quite a lot of research has now been done to find out the actual effects on young children of whether or not their mothers take jobs. Those who stay at home because they want to (and can afford to) do bring up normal happy children. But if they hate doing that, especially if they have training which they are no longer using, mothers suffer not only from fatigue, especially where there are a number of children, but most of all from the isolation – they have a need for human contact beyond that of their babies. Such conditions can cause young mothers to be unhappy, even depressed, and that is certainly not good for the children. There is evidence, collected in London by Dr George Brown, that some employment outside the home for mothers goes a long way towards relieving this distress.

Further findings collected by the married Doctors Rhona and Robert Rapaport showed that the children of working mothers did not often feel abandoned and unwanted, but were more likely to gain in feelings of independence and respect, with an enriched lifestyle, seeing their mothers as independent rather than dependent women. There does not seem to be any evidence of problems for the children caused specifically by their mothers' outside work. The real problems in the lives of young children with working mothers occur when the mothers are working because they are poor; it is the effects of the poverty, not the work itself, that cause the problems.

A mother's constant presence for the first five years of a child's life – the concern of the 1950s – is not now seen by psychologists as essential for his well-being. Today the accumulated evidence all points to the greatest benefit accruing to the child who receives care from both parents, where possible, with fathers sharing the work and the pleasure. A baby can be parented at least as well by more than one person, assuming they have the same style and they make sure that he has all he needs in plenty of one-to-one contact.

Every couple has to work out their own answer to the question of whether the mother of small children should take work outside the home. Unfortunately, it often seems to be a compromise, with a price to be paid by the mother, regardless of her choice; mothers in full-time work can get desperately tired, those in part-time work may be passed by for promotion, and those who stay at home unwillingly can suffer from depression and frustration. The question to ask, perhaps, is which price is right for your family?

Parents with problems

Bright aware children are particularly sensitive to other people's feelings, especially those of their mothers and fathers. So when there's some tension brewing at home, they may be the first to know about it. But children are affected differently by what they feel, and they have their ups and downs, too, which can make it difficult to tell how they're being affected. Just like adults, a child may find problems weighing heavy one day but perk up the next.

Although there are children who seem to be able to cope when their parents aren't getting on well together, for many it can disrupt their lives so that they become unhappy. Then there are real problems. Boys seem to be particularly sensitive to parental distress, or at least they react to it more than girls, as an in-depth study on the Isle of Wight, directed by Professor Michael Rutter, discovered. It's the constant pull of strained relationships that does most of the damage, but sometimes parents can also blame their troubles on the child, who is merely reacting to their personal problems, and so the situation goes from bad to worse; 'If it wasn't for Janice', they might say, 'we'd be happy.' But it's more likely to be the parents' behaviour that affects the children rather than the other way round, so that when the parents' lives become more harmonious, then their children's behaviour, and their performance at school, very often improves.

What you can do for your family

- Keep your family to the size and spacing that you can afford, both emotionally and financially.
- Get close to your baby right from the beginning – or at least try. It can sometimes take a while for feelings to develop.
- Be 'parents' and not only friends to your children. They need some structure in their lives, and to know that they can depend on you.
- Priorities often have to change when you have children. For instance, can you give up some space in the house for the children to use as a playroom? Are you willing to live with the mess they create?
- Whether the mother works outside the home or not, the choice must be made by the couple together. Be as open and honest in your discussions as you can, or the underlying resentment in either parent can make family life less than pleasant.
- Constant absence from children by either parent is not good for their healthy balanced development. If your work is all-demanding, you may have to choose between cutting it down somewhat or bringing up your children in what may be in reality a one-parent (or almost a no-parent) family.

The way parents feel about each other affects the way they bring up their children. For example, when a child is reprimanded in a loving accepting home, then the child understands what it's for, without heavy emotional overtones. But when parents are under strain, the quality of their general care may suffer, so that punishment is given out arbitrarily, confusing the child, who can't always see what he's done to deserve it. Sometimes it swings the other way, though, and parents under strain can become over-protective.

Children most often react to strained relationships at home in one of two ways:

- By becoming over anxious. This anxiety often comes out as aggression, in the forms of bad behaviour. Demonstrations of anger can be learned by even the tiniest baby, who may discover that it's only when she gets really worked up to screaming point that she gets the attention she wants, while silence or whimpering get her nowhere.

- By becoming safety valves. Children can draw attention away from the real problem of family stress and on to themselves. They can, for example, seem to be unwell. Most parents recognise the tummy-ache before school as a sign of tension, but other more serious problems such as asthma or diabetes can also be signs of stress, and may vanish when the stress goes.

Unfortunately, parents have been known to justify their child's bad behaviour by claiming it's because he's too clever, saying that it's only natural for him to be disturbed in this 'mediocre' world. So when a clever child has a temper tantrum, or disturbs the other children in class, it's said to be excusable because he's bored. Frustration and boredom – which are common to most children at times – should never be used as a licence for bad behaviour.

When bright children have behaviour problems, the likelihood is that there are reasons behind it, and these need attention, not excuses.

Parents' expectations

As Charlie Brown, one of the most powerful philosophers of this century, put it, 'There's no heavier burden than a great potential.' Sometimes you can try too hard to produce a child whose excellence brings credit to you. Pride in one's children's achievements is only right and good, but should you find yourselves thinking and talking of little else, then it's time to sit back and consider why.

Parents can live 'through' their children by pushing them to reach standards they never achieved themselves, either because they weren't capable of it or because they didn't have the opportunity. But it's impossible for a child to live up to his parents' expectations all the time, and sometimes he will let them down. These little failures can give his confidence a knock, which wouldn't matter too much in the ordinary way of things. But when the child is under too much pressure to succeed, his lack of confidence can either make him try exceptionally hard to please or perhaps just make him give up. A child can be too 'good', can feel it necessary to conform too much, which may cause him to harbour feelings of resentment, perhaps for the rest of his life.

It's important for a child to have the freedom and self-esteem to fail, yet know that he's still OK in his parents' eyes. It's all part of learning. Try to bring about an atmosphere at home in which the child feels secure and

---

What you can do about family problems

- Be clear in what you are directing the child to do and how you feel about it – does 'Behave yourself' really mean 'Be quiet?' If it's quiet you're after, then say so, and say why.
- Each parent should avoid giving instructions that contradict the other's; it confuses a child and makes him anxious, so try to be consistent.
- Respect your child's integrity; trust him to mean well.
- Keep the atmosphere of the home as tension-free as you can, for example by keeping parental arguments out of children's hearing.
- Reassure the child of his rightful place in the family, and that you love him, whatever. Tell him this in words of one syllable.
- When you're wrong, admit it. Your saving face is always less important than the child's feelings, and what he's learning from you about life.

---

accepted for himself, whatever he might do. This doesn't mean removing all discipline – parents have a right to live, too – but being aware of what your child is able to cope with. Expectations should not be too high or too low, but just right.

POSITION IN THE FAMILY

It's still one of the mysteries of psychology why first-born children in a family are likely to be more intelligent, have a better facility with language, and are usually more successful in life than the others. The great turn-of-the-century scientist Francis Galton stumbled across this interesting fact when he investigated his fellow members of the Royal Society – a significant majority of them were first-born children. Since then very many studies of different groups, as varied as Italian professors, American astronauts and striptease dancers, have shown them all to contain more first-borns than could have been expected. Is it due to their inborn characteristics, or is it the way they're brought up? If first-borns, who are more successful than their brothers and sisters, have in fact been treated differently, that could provide some clues as to how they have been able to get ahead.

Being a first-born or, almost equally, being an only child, has a big effect on a child's intellectual and personality growth. Most studies of highly able individuals have found a higher than chance proportion of their being first-borns or only children. An intriguing study by Eleanor Maccoby and her colleagues found that first-borns are born with a higher level of hormones in their blood than later-born children, especially if the pregnancies are closely spaced. We don't yet know, though, what the implications of this finding are. Sometimes last-borns also do well, but middle-borns are usually the least successful children. Even though their differences in intelligence are real – when measured across large numbers of people – they still cannot entirely account for the spectacularly high rate of success among first-borns.

In an important study of 400,000 young men conscripted into the Dutch Army, the results showed that the higher a soldier was in his family birth order, the higher his intelligence score was likely to be. It also showed that the larger the family, the lower the intelligence of the younger children was likely to be. Other studies, such as that by Dr Douglas in Britain, have also found that children from large families often don't do as well as those from smaller ones. In big poor families, where everyone is crowded into a small home and there isn't enough money for books or learning activities, the children's full mental growth can't always take place. The greater the strain on a family's resources of attention, care and interest, the less each subsequent child is likely to receive of them; the first-born is always likely to scoop the lion's share.

There is also evidence showing that most first-borns do have a different upbringing from later-borns. During the time in which they are the only children they command all their parents' attention, something later children never experience, although they are also in an experimental position for their parents' new childraising skills. This means that they arrive into a very different style of family life from later-born children. New parents – mothers in particular – also often have higher expectations for their first baby than they do for the others; accordingly mothers give much more help and encouragement to their first child than they do to the later ones, and fathers probably do the same.

The extra attention which the first-born receives – mostly in his first two years – carries over into his later relationship with his parents, though in different forms. Parents are not quite as easy-going with their first baby as they will be with the rest. Perhaps this is because, as new parents, they are unused to handling babies and so often describe their first-born as less cuddly than the later-borns. Still, in spite of this possible lack of cuddling, first-borns do get more attention than later-borns. They more often model themselves on their parents than later-borns, who are more likely to follow their friends. As first-borns tend to be more considerate, too, they can seem to be more 'old-fashioned' and grown-up than other children.

The typical first-born is clever and well behaved. She does her best to please, but may also let you know that she's doing you a favour. She's a bit anxious about life in general and finds it hard to relax, so her leisure time is taken up with fairly 'educational' hobbies such as collecting stamps, from which she can learn a lot. When she's with other children, she usually thinks she knows best, since she sees herself more as a grown-up than a child. Grown-ups are more likely to treat her as one of themselves, so they are less likely to talk down to her, even when she's very tiny. She will probably take more responsibility than the other children of the family, which seems to be right, since she's usually a more 'responsible' child. The best card she has to play is her own success; the first astronauts to set foot on the moon were all first-borns, and it's very likely that the child at the top of the class will be one too.

Only children may do even better at school and in intelligence tests than first-borns, as they often aim higher

What you can do about position in the family

- Space your family so that each child can get plenty of attention when they are very tiny. With generous spacing between births, say three or four years, each baby can almost be a first-born for a while, though children born closer together can often benefit more later on from each other's companionship.
- Try especially hard to give the later-born children what you gave the first. Obviously this is not entirely possible, but you can try to avoid the snare of giving relatively less and less attention to each child that comes. To make sure, you could keep a rough written checklist on what you do for each one.

and are more ambitious. Although it seems paradoxical, only children have both a higher level of self-confidence, and yet are more dependent on being told what to do and on parents' and teachers' opinions.

It's often said that middle children have to struggle to keep their end up in a family, and this is true. They do receive less attention than any others in the family, and seem to feel this lack for much of their lives. When they're little they'll often go to great lengths to make their presence felt, even if it results in punishment. They can be particularly quarrelsome and obstinate, and are often the least popular members of the family. It's unlikely that they will ever do as well as the first-born, since their drive to succeed is usually much lower.

Children's popularity with their friends is also affected by their position in the family. First children, so grown-up and sometimes 'know-all', are the least popular. Middle children usually have as many friends as they want, but last-born children hit the top of the popularity ratings – their teachers show them the same warmth as friends of their own age do. Right through from kindergarten, last-borns are always the most attractive to teachers, and first-borns the least attractive.

THE VALUE OF CHILDREN'S FRIENDS

It's important for all children's emotional development, and therefore their intellectual development too, to have friends. Children who haven't got many friends find it much harder to grow up as well-balanced adults. Psychologists have found that children learn a lot about how to behave and cope with life through their friends.

Bright children usually have sympathy, adaptability and compassion in abundance, and don't usually choose to be without friends. They can expect to have the same number and depths of friendships as all the other children at school, but they're sometimes less eager to spend time playing with them at home. The reason is often that there's so much they want to do after school. Many lively children use that time to enjoy their hobbies, or they may practise a musical instrument. After that, there's supper, maybe a little television, and then bed. And there's another day gone.

Whether they're especially bright or not, children in mixed ability classes at school normally pick friends across a wide mental range. And it's the same at home, where they will normally play happily with any others. But sometimes parents give their children the idea that they're quite different (if not superior) and expect them to spend their time more purposefully than in ordinary play. The kind of 'differences' that parents choose to impose on their children are many and varied, cleverness being only one of them, and they give the message in very subtle ways. For example, a mother might say 'Oh, so you want to play with Johnny . . . He's a bit quiet for you, isn't he?', or she may just pull a disapproving face at the mention of children who don't meet with her approval.

Some people say that particularly able children don't make friends of their own age easily because they get bored and frustrated with children who have a lower level of understanding. Although there may be a problem when a child is very much in advance of his age group, this isn't usual, nor is it unsolvable if it arises. If clever children don't seem to want to make friends with others of their own age, it can be for two reasons. The first is their high level of self-sufficiency, which means that they're happier on their own for longer periods of time than other children, but the other reason is that they may have been 'put off' playing with other children by their parents' unspoken, but understood, disapproval.

Parents' fears of the bad influences of friends are not usually justified. Friends help children to see life from another's point of view, so that they can learn more about concern for others and discover that their friends might have similar problems with grown-ups. Furthermore, criticism as well as support are often more acceptable to a child when they come from friends. The rough and tumble of learning to make and break their own relationships not only helps children find out about themselves; it also teaches them the skills they need for working and living with other people – something that is as important for bright children as for any others.

Younger children often enjoy playing with older children and usually imitate them, so older children can often be very good teachers for younger ones. Some schools take advantage of this, especially when children first start school, by putting the older ones in charge. The old-timers can then teach the newcomers about how to behave in school, not to mention helping them get ready to go home.

There are children who could be described as 'socially gifted'. They have lots of friends and seem to be unusually

---

What you can do about friends

- From about a year old, make sure your child mixes with other babies. They won't play together yet, but they'll get used to having each other around.
- Help your toddler learn to share toys and adult attention by encouraging it patiently and gently. The message will get through in time.
- Respect your child's choice of friends, though it may be surprising, or even hard at times. It's part of your respect for your child as a person.
- Try not to be too protective; children learn about other children from their own mistakes, and don't always appreciate an adult's point of view as to who it is worth being friends with.
- Clever children do take special pleasure in meeting others who are like them. Don't we all? If you child is really without equally able children to play with in her local group, try to help her get to know one or two, even if they live further away, and try to find some out-of-school activities for bright children that she could join in with.

sensitive in understanding other children's feelings. Such children very often turn out to be leaders, though they aren't necessarily more intelligent than their followers.

ABOUT SLEEP

Highly able children are sometimes said to need less sleep than other children. If this were true, then their parents could anticipate it and learn how to deal with it, but as yet there isn't any evidence to support the idea. However, there is plenty of evidence to show that children's sleep habits are very much influenced by their parents' approach to bringing them up.

As they grow older, both the length of time children sleep and their wakefulness during the night become less. Children do vary in this respect, though, not only as individuals but in terms of their families. When they were studying the daily routines of babies in England, Lawson and Ingleby found that what was considered to be 'normal' sleeping time varied by a difference of hours between families. 'Normal' waking-up time for toddlers was seen as any time between 6 and 10.30 am, and the time for going to sleep varied from 5.30 to 11 pm. They noticed that first-born babies were put to bed less often during the day than later-born babies, and that they slept less too. There were also social-class differences; the higher the social class, the longer the baby was expected to sleep, and both going to sleep and waking were earlier in the day. Other researchers, such as Professor Richards in Cambridge, found that parents were not able to alter children's sleep patterns no matter what they did – the children just seemed to be born with a particular sleep pattern.

Parents' feelings about what constitutes a sleep problem depend very much on their attitudes. If they are relatively easy-going in their approach, the child may be given toys and books to play with and allowed late bedtimes, and it is less likely that a problem will develop. But if they feel strongly about their responsibility to instil good sleeping habits, then by six o'clock the child may be required to lie

What you can do about sleep

- Keep bedtime as calm and regular as possible. About half of all children between the ages of one and two make a great fuss at bedtime; try to ride the storm calmly, being both reassuring and firm.
- All children wake several times during the night and fall asleep again. Don't go into your child's room constantly to see if he's all right, or you may disturb his natural rhythm and set up expectations and demands. For instance, each time you go in he may wake and want to be taken into your bed; don't start this, or you'll regret it.
- Try to judge how much sleep a child really needs, rather than going by a book that says how much time he 'should' sleep.
- Put just enough (but not too many) interesting toys in the cot for a child to play with when he's wakeful; you can tie them on to the side when he's little. Provide more involving things, like cloth books, when he gets older. (See pages 34 and 47 for cot toys.)
- Try not to make an issue of sleep; it will only make matters worse.
- Parents need time to themselves too. Children can understand from an early age that once they are comfortable and have something to do in bed, then you have a right to a breather.

still, stop reading, be quiet, etc. Lawson and Ingleby found a significant proportion of parents in Britain who did just that every night, and if the child wasn't ready for sleep when they believed he should be, they were likely to regard it as a problem.

In fact almost all children have sleep problems at some time, and about half of all parents worry about whether their children are getting enough sleep. The problems with sleep come at particularly anxious periods in their lives, such as the birth of another baby in the house, starting school, separation from mother or strained relations between parents. Babies' sleep patterns affect their growing relationship with their parents. For example, if a baby doesn't sleep as expected, parents may become frustrated and pass angry feelings back to the infant.

Unfortunately, some children are just poor sleepers from the time they are born. These children, perfectly normal in all other respects, may have some history in common. They're often born after long labours, and have been rather fussy and wakeful from birth. On average, they spend less time in bed than other children, but it doesn't seem to do them any harm. Parents of poor sleepers may try many things, such as changing feeding times or giving more cuddling and attention, but it usually doesn't influence the sleeplessness. Not even the parents' attitudes towards the child seem to make any difference. What can happen is that a constant battle ensues, in which everyone, apart from the baby, suffers from lack of sleep. Some parents alter their lives to fit in with a baby's choice of sleep times – for example, getting up at 3 am for playtime. That's dedication – or madness, depending on your point of view.

HOW COMPETENCE DEVELOPS

Competence – being able to cope – is an essential part of every child's learning. Though it's difficult to describe, we all know it when we see it. It means taking the right action at the right time; it means making things happen, as well as seeing them through in the right way. Children learn how to be competent, and learn the self-esteem that goes with it, within their families.

Babies soon learn the effects they can have on their world, and at the same time begin to learn how to value themselves. During his first year a baby comes to realise that he exists independently of other people and that he's different from them; it's then he begins to get a glimmer of the understanding of the word 'me'. That's why parents should answer the baby's crying and calls as much as they can, because his growing sense of self-worth comes from his communication with others. Though a child only really sees himself as an individual member of the family from about three years old, he's been striving to get there for a long time. When you're two years old, you're small and unable to think very far ahead, so the best stab you can make at independence is just to say 'no' to everything.

It's when the baby begins to recognise familiar people from strangers, at about six months, that you can see his first stirrings of independence. As soon as he begins to crawl he will explore around, when he's confident that Mummy and Daddy will be there all the time. Babies start exploring when they're ready; parents can't push them into it, though they can pave the way. Play with your baby and make encouraging noises when he reaches out for something. Tell him how well he's doing, as long as it is safe; it gives him the courage to try a bit more. Wherever he is, the room has to be reasonably baby-proof, or parents spend their time saying 'No, don't touch', which isn't good for anyone.

Sometimes it is the parents' own feelings of insecurity that won't allow them to help their baby find his way around. How often do over-anxious mothers say 'Don't do that; you'll hurt yourself', whether it's likely or not. This certainly puts a brake on the baby's exploring for a while. Adults who let the baby know he's helpless and useless can undermine both his confidence and his ability to use his inner resources when he needs them; in effect, they can slow up his thinking this way. Every step forward a baby takes, every new friendship, every meeting with a new idea, can add to his feelings about himself and his growing competence. This isn't only a matter of parents trying to give their children confidence in themselves, but means showing them ways of doing things, and involving them in the process. Children's intellectual development is very closely tied to their emotional state; parents who help them cope are also helping them to do better in life.

Here are two examples of the way competence-building works.

- While waiting in a supermarket checkout recently I was able to watch a complete interaction of a mother and her little boy of about four years old. It was a demonstration of how to cut down a child's communication skills. I noticed them when the child demanded chewing gum very persistently. At last his mother gave in, but then ignored him while he tore off the wrapping and dropped it on the clean floor. Then the little boy tried to talk to her, but at first she wouldn't listen. 'Speak up', she said eventually, 'I can't hear you when you mumble.' So the child did speak up. 'Don't shout,' the mother said, 'I'm not deaf.' He stopped talking and chewed his gum in glum silence.

- Four year old Mary's problem had a happier ending. She'd been given a simple train set for her birthday, but it took up all the floor space in her room. Mary and her parents put their heads together. Father, who'd twisted his ankle on it, wanted it put away at night; Mother, who had a feeling for tidiness, tended to agree with him, though she understood Mary's feelings too. It was Mary who, at the last minute, saw that moving the bed along the wall would solve the problem. Her initiative was rewarded by her parents' sincere expressions of delight at her competence, and she then had the train set out all the time. She'll use her head again when she needs to. Smart girl.

What you can do to help develop competence

- Give your baby lots of opportunities to try out his new coping skills. 'Educational' toys like putting rings on a peg are valuable for babies; later on, friendships become more important, so see that he has companions and meets people. *Toys and Playthings* by John and Elizabeth Newson (see

reading list on page 175) is very helpful on
choosing worthwhile toys, and there are certainly
plenty to buy.

- Encourage a child to understand what he's doing
and why; it develops his self-understanding and
mental growth. You can do this from a very early
age by talking about what you and he are doing,
and trying different approaches, such as 'Let's see
what happens if you shake it.'

- Reward good behaviour when it happens, rather
than simply giving in to constant demands to gain
a moment's peace. For example, when your child's
been noticeably good by 'helping' with the
washing-up, reward him with a kiss or something
nice, and say thank you. But if he screams for
chocolate at the supermarket checkout, where it is
usually temptingly on display, don't give in; it only
encourages him to scream again next time.

- Keep the idea of learning as a pleasure, so that you
don't use the word 'no' more than you can help.
Encourage the baby's natural feeling for exploring,
and enjoy taking part in his explorations yourself.

- Little children can be given simple tools so that
they can learn how to use them under supervision.
Competence in potentially dangerous activities,
like handling hammers and nails, and knowing
how to swim, is far better than trying to put the
damage to rights afterwards.

- Babies need balance in their interests. By the time
a baby is a year old the mother should try to get a
free and easy relationship going with him. The
baby will then have the confidence to let his
mother out of his sight from time to time, and take
a wider interest in other things. Otherwise, she
could end up with a two-year-old nagger.

5 THE MAKING OF MINDS

Mind and body have such a very close working relationship that one hardly ever acts without the other – they both interact with and affect each other all the time. Thoughts and emotions from the mind are needed for body movements to take place (except for automatic reflexes); for example, the brain area that deals with leg movements needs the cooperation of the mind in providing the wish to move. On a different level, breaking a leg can make you feel depressed.

Whenever we humans use our minds and bodies, we do it rather in the way we've learned since birth, by having to fit in and cope with the world that we are part of. The human mind has a natural tendency to put some order into what's going on around it. We actually enjoy sorting and classifying and making rules about life – listen to any toddler as he discovers these joys. Many of the personal rules we make up don't seem to have any real purpose, or to make sense, but are just a sort of intellectual exercise.

We like to make forbidding rules too; a group of children making up a game can sort out a hundred 'dos' and 'don'ts' in no time. But the negative rules often have an emotional basis in fear, such as 'Don't walk under a ladder' or 'Don't walk on the cracks.' It is fear that causes people to conform so that they can avoid emotional conflict, though paradoxically it is through some conflict in ideas that we grow and learn intellectually and become creative.

It is good to be able to report that human beings have the highest form of intelligence in the animal world – or, at least, so we believe. Among all the warm-blooded creatures, only people have the ability to be self-reflexive – to talk to themselves. And communication is the true key to the development of the mind. It's not that animals do not communicate, but they are rather restricted in their language, and it is particularly in the use of words that the human mind develops.

In its broadest sense, intelligence is the individual's power to cope with their personal world. It's about reaching your goals, whether basic, like finding enough to eat, or more distant, like passing an exam. Intelligence works by assessing what is available and then taking the best possible actions on the basis of that understanding.

One can draw a comparison between intelligence and physical ability. Although practice can make a big difference to athletic performance, some people find that they can win races relatively easily while others trail along at the end, no matter how hard they try. Psychologists would be overjoyed to have the key to increasing greatly the power of people's mental abilities, but no one has yet come up with the magic formula. You still can't make a silk purse out of a sow's ear.

However, although intelligence can't be boosted

dramatically, at the other extreme it can certainly be stopped from growing to its full potential. Very severe physical conditions, such as brain damage at birth, or early starvation, can damage its growth. Children reared in isolation from other people, by deranged adults for instance, have very limited mental abilities unless they are rescued early. But more subtly, the effects of an intellectually poor upbringing can pull down a child's level of mental functioning to below his natural level.

In measuring intelligence it is obviously important to be aware of what is cultural, but it is also important to include everyday intelligence where possible, because intelligence always refers to the real world and what is valued in it. Whatever components go to make up this most tantalising of human abilities, it has to be seen in its natural habitat.

After a century's investigations into the nature of intelligence, people may be forgiven for thinking that psychologists still don't know their own minds. But there is such a thing as intelligence – it's not a myth, and it need not be a mystery either. The problem is that intelligence cannot be measured as a clearcut mental power in the same way that, say, physical power can be measured by the weight of dumb-bells lifted. There are so many aspects to intelligence that each test can only measure parts of it, and we're not sure how the tests overlap. Perhaps it is easiest to think of intelligence as a shapeless moving collection of different thinking abilities, such as reasoning, critical judgment, flexibility of mind and original thinking, which all work together. Different statistical methods have produced over 100 different kinds of thinking abilities, though the margin between them is sometimes too small to be seen by the 'naked eye'.

LANGUAGE

One of the earliest forms of language, both for the human race and for each baby, is giving a name to things. Even now, naming has some magical qualities which our more primitive ancestors would have recognised. Some religions, such as orthodox Judaism for example, refuse to name their god for fear of what might happen. The 'doing' words usually come next in order of importance, and then words for more abstract ideas.

Children have to learn the sounds and meanings of whatever language is spoken by their parents, and they also acquire the thought processes that have developed in that language over the centuries of its use. In this way, children's thoughts and behaviour are inextricably bound up with the use of language. For example, a child's simple demand 'Pick me up' tells us a lot about her mental activity – that she sees herself as distinct from other people, believes in her own power of command, and that she associates the physical act of being lifted with particular emotional needs and responses.

The way we use words provides a good indication of the way our minds work. Thought has to be put into words so that it can be communicated; and for it to be put into words, it first has to be sorted into categories. First we think, and then we want to say what we think, to express it somehow. In a living growing culture new words are born, while others fade from lack of use. Before 1960 no one would have understood the words 'laid-back' or 'swinging' in the way they subsequently came to be used; now they are out of fashion, indeed quite dated. And, of course, we don't always understand the archaic words that television quiz shows, for example, dig up as teasers – words such as 'loafers', 'swells' or 'bounders'; the usefulness of these words as conveyors of ideas has long since passed away. Language that is alive is always open to change, and we who speak it are changing it all the time.

Learning to talk is probably the single most important part of a child's intellectual development. It begins from birth with the 'conversations' between mothers and their babies (as described in Chapter 3). Parents who are generous in listening and responding to their babies are starting them firmly on the right path to good language development. The better this kind of intellectual parenting has been, the greater the baby's intellectual development.

Fortunately, babies have an inborn grasp of language, which makes it easy for them to learn quickly. By four years old, children are so proficient in their language that they can help younger ones learn to speak, and even simplify their language so that it can be better understood.

To help a baby develop language ability, it's essential for parents to spend as much time as they can in conversation with him. The baby's babbling or first stumbling efforts to talk should be listened to very carefully and then answered, as far as possible, in a way that the baby is able to take in. To do this it's important to speak directly to him at eye-to-eye level. But babies still go on learning, even when you aren't talking to them.

A child can only improve her talking when she's ready for it; you can't force-feed language, because the baby just won't accept it. For example, a baby who is two months old can imitate and learn to use vowel sounds, but she can't manage consonants yet. She'll begin to pick them up in another couple of months, though. The baby's first year of language learning holds a number of keys to her later talking and thinking abilities. For example, her early babblings contain all the sounds she is going to use as a child. They may even give an idea of how intelligent the child is going to be; heavy babblers often grow up to be clever children, for example. On the other hand it can be disappointing that babies who can speak before they're expected to don't necessarily grow up to be more articulate or clever, because very early speech is more like imitation than considered utterances.

The most striking, and probably the most effective, difference between the experience of bright and less bright children is in the amount of conversation their families make, both with the baby and with each other. This applies not only to the amount, of course, but to the quality also. It's in the family setting that a child learns to use language to express his ideas and, in using it, develops a style of intellectual activity.

Much of what we understand through our senses – especially hearing and seeing – comes about because of the way we were brought up to use language. When there isn't much talk in a home, thoughts and ideas stand much less of a chance to be practised and to develop. But a high level of conversation within the family does not automatically result in early speech. Many famous people didn't start to speak until they were well into childhood; Churchill's early difficulties with speaking gave no indication of his later brilliant spoken and written English.

It can help you to get a true picture of your baby's talking if you keep a simple record of what she can say. She may start out by sounding some consonants like 'r' and 'p' from around six months, and from then till she's about a year old her babbling usually goes on at a great rate. A baby is quite likely to have a few words in hand by the time she's a year old, and then she moves on swiftly.

Babies begin by giving names to what they see around them every day – usually moveable things. They often start with food and drink, then go on to animals, clothes and toys. Nowadays, a baby is more likely to say 'car' before 'house'. At 14 to 20 months, mothers still need to name things for the child; if she says 'doll' in an expectant voice, the baby will try to repeat it. But she should keep the pressure on – as soon as he seems to master that one, she can test him, asking 'What is it?' Her expectations should be just a little ahead of what he's managed to do so far.

Between 18 months and two years old, babies start to put words together, like 'Daddy go car'. It's the beginning of grammar, but they've still got a way to go. Then, as the child's talking develops, she begins to move away from the here-and-now, so that she can begin to tell her listener something, and ask simple questions. Parents can help by asking her 'What did you do? What did you see?'

Each group of people, even a group as small as a family, has its own rules about language, and the child has to learn to fit in with them. He starts by learning the general way people around him speak and think, then tightens up on the rules as he is corrected. For example, an adult might say 'Would you be so kind as to post this letter?' But the speaker is not really asking the listener to outline his degree of kindness; what appears grammatically to be a question is really a demand, wrapped up in convention, and this is the way language is actually used. A child's sensitivity to the way adults think helps him to learn the rules of language; this goes for the later learning of foreign languages too.

When they make mistakes in speaking, children are still going by rules, such as saying 'He hurted me.' The rule there used in this example is indeed the one that would be expected, but English usage often has to be learned word by word, outside the rules. By five years old, children have learned those rules so well that they can speak with hardly a mistake. But the more practice and attention children have in language learning, the better they will be at it.

In everyday conversations, even with very tiny children, parents can use language to help enlarge a child's ideas about the topic of the moment. A simple example might go as follows.

Jimmy (aged 3) I'm going to be a fireman when I grow up.
Mother A fireman, hmm. So you can put out lots of fires with great big hoses.
Jimmy I'll splash water everywhere.
Mother (teasingly) Then you might not have enough left to put out the fire.
Jimmy Well, I'll put out most of the fire.

If Jimmy's original idea hadn't been taken up at this point, he probably wouldn't have gone on to consider how much water it would take to put the fire out. This exchange, though tiny, has notched another peg in Jimmy's understanding. But giving ideas and information is an art; if Jimmy's mother had begun to list aspects of fire-fighting, in an attempt to teach him too much, the likelihood is that he would have switched off and learned very little.

To have the greatest learning effect, topics of conversation must be interesting to the child and should only go on for as long as she shows interest. You can tell what a little baby is interested in by seeing how long she looks at something. Then you can talk about it to her, even before she can speak – babies can understand meaning long before they can talk. As children get older, their conversations get longer and more complicated, but they will let you know when they've had enough of a topic.

Children don't learn to speak by parrot-like imitation; they learn best in pleasurable social situations, where they can practise what they already know, and go on to try a bit more. Showing pleasure at your baby's efforts to make sounds gives her the encouragement to go on learning. Intelligent listening will always be one of the most important presents that parents can give a child.

Talking to a baby is not just a watered-down version of talking to an adult. You're not only communicating, you're also teaching, all the time. The more the baby's language improves, the more scope he has for learning more. Language can be self-generating.

Speaking to babies or little children

- Repeat what you say.
- Keep to the here-and-now.
- Speak quite loudly.
- Be clear in your pronunciation.
- Ask simple questions.
- Don't try too hard to teach by presenting too much information.

Children's questions

As they get older, children begin to ask questions, but brighter children ask different kinds from the others. Ordinary children ask more 'What' questions, like 'What's that thing called?' or 'Where is my teddy?', but the bright child asks more 'Why?' questions, such as 'Why is the moon in the sky?' These 'Why?' questions are often more difficult to answer, sometimes even impossible, but they come from a searching growing intelligence and shouldn't be answered in a patronising or offhand way.

Parents should try to answer 'Why?' questions in as impersonal a way as a child can accept at that age. This helps her to think outwards from her own tiny world into a more abstract way of thinking and reasoning. Unfortunately, parents who feel unsure about their own ability to answer these (sometimes deep-sounding) questions often try to avoid answering them factually. Yet the child's own understanding is very limited and she really needs the information, such as in this example:

Mother It's four o'clock.
Annie (aged 3) Why is it four o'clock?
Mother Because your tea's ready.
Annie (Silence.)

A better response to Annie would have been for her mother to say:

Well, when we had dinner, it was one o'clock; then we went shopping so the clock went one, two, three, and now it's four o'clock, and time for tea.
Annie I like four o'clock.

Children are constantly on the lookout, trying to understand what's going on. When they come to events and remarks which don't make sense to them, they should feel free to ask about them. They are always working towards building up a picture of what they see, but they suspect they might not have it right, so they are always vulnerable to a put-down. Children's questions are almost always serious (though they sometimes get out of hand when the children find that it's a good way of getting extra attention).

A problem with children's questioning is that they can't always express themselves very clearly, and may ask questions that are misleading, especially if parents aren't listening very carefully. Children can believe, for example, that television characters are real, or they may not understand adult social customs, like paying a bill – 'Is Bill a window cleaner? Do you only pay one Bill? Are all window cleaners called Bill? Why doesn't Bill pay you?' Their questions may be perfectly logical, within the limits

What you can do about language
For babies:

- Keep physically close to a baby; talk and listen as much as you feel she is happy with.
- Offer your baby simple things like a toy and a comb, and see which he looks at. Then pick this object up and show it to him; 'talk' about it together. Show him other things in the house in the same way.
- When your baby is about a year old, teach him to point to things and name them.
- Recite nursery rhymes with clear rhythm and pleasure.
- Read to him and show him the pictures in books, starting from when he is only a few months old.
- See if the few words your baby knows have anything in common – shape, colour or texture. Show him similar things, and talk about what's the same and what's different.
- Keep using the same words and phrases, so that your baby gets to know the sound of them.
- Encourage the baby to take the lead in conversation, and to take pleasure in it.

For toddlers:

- Praise effort, and don't correct grammar too often.
- Keep 'baby talk' to a minimum.
- Use the same 'key' words over and over again.
- Describe things that are physically present, so that he can coordinate all that he can hear, see, touch and smell.
- Keep your conversation as lively and interesting to the child as possible.
- Help the child use the words he already knows.
- Answer properly not just by saying 'Oh'. It's conversation you're after.

of their knowledge. What may appear to be ridiculous questioning may not be childish or attention-seeking, but the efforts of a bright child who has worked something out (if incorrectly) and who wants to know more.

Children need time to work through their own thoughts, and it helps to encourage this intellectual curiosity. An only child gets much more opportunity to do this than a child with brothers and sisters. Parents and children also need to have built up a certain trust in order for the child to feel able to try out strange new paths of thought. This comes about through plenty of shared experience. Spending their days together helps parents to understand their child; long periods of separation such as being in hospital can make it much more difficult.

Bright children often have a lively sense of humour too – even babies can have a mischievous sense of fun – which anxious adults can miss. I once heard a bright five year old ask 'What's the difference between a dinosaur's bone and a chicken bone?' The serious adults considered various educated answers – was it evolutionary, was it the difference between birds and reptiles? They all gave different answers. 'Wrong,' came the reply, 'One's smaller.'

Music

The ability to take pleasure in and to perform music always adds to the liveliness of a child's mental and emotional development. As always, it is what parents do, the example they set, rather than the instructions they give, which have the most effect. Musical education can start from birth, with the rhythm in parents' singing and in rocking movements.

There is no shortage of music anywhere in the world. Let your baby and other children hear all kinds of music, from classical through folk songs to jazz. Try, too, to see that children experience music that does not come through an electronic outlet. There are concerts in parks, bands marching through the streets, and usually a guitar or a piano somewhere around.

When my children used to come home from school tired,

What to do with music

- Make singing as much a part of the bedtime routine as story-telling.
- Sing with fidgety children in cars, and to and from school or on journeys. Even tiny babies will try to coo along.
- Teach other things with music, such as 'This is the way we wash our hands'. It helps little children to concentrate on the words and remember them. However, I learned my alphabet to the tune of 'Twinkle Twinkle Little Star', with a repeated bit in the middle. When I am tired I sometimes still have to repeat that middle section to get to the next part, because I have to complete the tune.
- Sing stories instead of speaking them.
- Movement is a visualised response to sound, so, as Fred Astaire used to sing, 'Lets start the music and dance'. Make it wild or happy, sad or elegant.
- Most babies' first musical instrument is a rattle, in most cultures of the world. You can soon move him on to others, though, such as two old pan lids or wooden blocks to clap together, or a toy drum to bang loudly.
- Let children choose their own music, however it sounds to you. As with books, the excitement of choosing makes it especially personal and meaningful for the child.

and sometimes less than chirpy, I would play tuneful rhythmic music (admittedly on audio-tapes), such as Strauss waltzes or disco, and we would dance and sing together till we all felt better. I recommend it.

BRAIN AND MIND

Both the physical make-up of the brain and the way it operates affect a person's intelligence. For our purposes the brain can be thought of as a highly complicated switchboard in a telephone system (though one big difference is that thought messages are transmitted almost immediately). It operates by using special nerve cells, called neurones, which are densely packed together. These neurones each have fibres that link up with fibres of other neurones, forming a complex network. Each neurone can store images, which are taken in and sent on to other neurones by an electric current that jumps across a gap (synapse) between their fibres.

Thinking is the result of up to 10 billion neurones constantly exchanging information. Just one neurone can probably connect with as many as 1,000 others at the same time; the more information-passing fibres a neurone has, the greater its ability to transmit information. In theory, there is no limit to the amount of material the brain can cope with. On that basis, if we could increase the branching of the information-giving fibres, we could improve intelligence. One hypothesis is that very intelligent people have more of these branching fibres than the less intelligent, which would explain how they can process information so much more efficiently. Another is that the more a child uses a particular nerve route, the quicker the synapse gap is jumped, in which case mental exercises such as mental arithmetic or lively discussion should be beneficial.

Psychological research on rats has shown that the thicker the fatty coating around each nerve fibre, the quicker they conduct information and the more intelligently the rats behave. This thickness was found to increase when the rats were handled more by their keepers and also when they were given a more stimulating task – in the rats' case, this took the form of a more complicated maze to negotiate. It is quite possible that human information-processing is similarly affected. So, if we transfer these findings to children, it would follow that intelligence – or at least speed of thought – could be nurtured through physical affection and a stimulating learning environment.

The brain is something of a computer, too, as it seems to operate mostly on procedures similar to computer programs, the information that the nerve cells store either being in individual bits or in chains. A simple body action, such as raising a little finger, simultaneously triggers off millions of circuits in the brain – all exactly the right ones for the job. Whatever we learn is stored in programs for further use, but, as we are human beings and not computers, our brains tend to use these programs in an emotional way. For example, we are not keen to take in new learning unless it seems interesting or rewarding. In other words, we learn best what we want to learn.

Bright children can cope with more complicated programs than others, and can use their better mental facilities of memory and concentration to develop new ideas. Parents can encourage their children to develop storage capacity by being positive and giving praise for good memory, instead of offering the more usual put-down remarks for forgetfulness, such as 'You'd forget your head if it wasn't screwed on.' You could also use memory improvement games; for example, Kim's game is fun, as well as being an excellent learning-to-learn game.

Kim's game

Put a selection of small objects, such as a rubber band, doll's shoe, a toy teacup and a little box, on a tray, then cover it with a cloth. Do this without the children watching. The show the covered tray to the children, take the cloth off for five seconds, cover it again and get the children to draw what they remember of it. Count up how many things they've remembered, and give a score, too, for whether they've put them in the right positions, as well as for how well they've drawn them.

The way the brain works is also influenced by hormones. These are body chemicals, made by glands around the body, which affect our body functions, especially our emotions. For example, if a child has a negative attitude to what he's supposed to be learning, or is bored, frightened or tired, the thymus gland gives off hormones (endorphins) which can actually block new information getting to the highest levels of brain processing. Exam 'nerves' are an example of the action of fear and hormones; you may have faced an exam paper and found that you couldn't remember a thing, and although you struggled valiantly to put something down, even answers which you knew perfectly the day before seemed to have vanished. One way of overcoming this problem in children's learning is to try to keep it interesting and tension-free, and to give lots of praise so that they feel good about it. Don't try to cram material into tired children; they are not empty vessels waiting to be filled, but eager learners, ready for the revelations you will provide.

Right brain and left brain

For centuries, great thinkers have written about the split between thinking based on reason and that based on emotion. But it is only since the late 1950s that psychologists, particularly Robert Ornstein in America, have discovered that this differentiation is due to the different influences of the two physical halves of the brain. It began with observing epileptics and patients who'd had brain injuries, where either the two halves of the brain had become separated or there was damage to specific parts of the brain.

People who are dominated in their thinking by the right half of their brain tend to see things as a whole. They are concerned with patterns, shapes and sizes, and are more imaginative and intuitive. Their ideas can seem vague and woolly to left-brain dominated people, who are often better at more logical and academic work such as mathematics and word skills. Whereas the right side will help you to hum a tune, write a poem or see a painting as a whole, the left side will help you to write grammatically, mend an engine, or admire the brush technique of the artist. But for most people, the two halves work together in harmony. The brain is not so much one computer but two, working together for better effect.

It seems that the seeds of knowledge are largely absorbed in gulps by the more spontaneous right brain, and then they are sorted out and communicated by the left brain. Each half can do the other's work to some extent, but functions better when the incoming information fits its style of processing. It isn't always the appropriate half, though, that tackles incoming information. Most people have a bias to one side, which gives them their special style, but which can interfere with aspects of their learning. For example, poor spellers may be biased to use their right brain more than their left, so they rely too much on their intuition and don't pay enough attention to the details of the letters.

Babies and toddlers don't usually have a dominant half to their brain, but traditional teaching in schools has emphasized the more rigid left-brain activity, sometimes to the detriment of the right, so that conformity is usually more dominant by the time children leave school. Indeed, school and IQ tests seem designed more for the left brain than the right. Some psychologists even believe that if certain right-brain activities are not exercised regularly, they will never develop properly. Since the greatest creative achievements require both halves of the brain, an overly academic education can cut down a child's creative potential. Therefore, teachers have begun lately to cultivate the more intuitive creative right brain. The accompanying box contains a couple of short lists of the ways in which children who are dominated by one side or the other are likely to behave.

It is possible that there are sex differences in right- and left-brain use. Girls are usually said to be dominated by the right brain, being intuitive. Boys are said to be left-brain dominated, and so better at mathematics and engineering. But as babies do not show any signs of this specialisation,

Characteristics of children dominated by one or the other side of the brain

Left Brain
- Likes formal teaching
- Is persistent.

- Is responsible.

- Is happy learning alone.

- Stays still while learning
- Does well at school.

Right brain
- Likes low lights and warmth.
- Not keen to sit and learn.
- Likes learning in company.
- Likes moving around, touching and doing things.
- Doesn't do brilliantly at school.

which increases as children get older, it is very likely that it is the way each sex is brought up that influences their style of thinking. Any child can get into lopsided thinking habits. Parents can watch out for this and try to correct the balance, to help the child stay mentally agile.

Another way of looking at this division of thinking styles is to group children as 'divergent' or 'convergent' thinkers. This corresponds pretty well with right- and left-brain thinkers respectively. A convergent thinker goes by the rules, will probably reach conclusions quite logically and generally does well in scientific and mathematical activities. Divergent thinkers are more creative, coming up with new and maybe crazy-sounding ideas and approaches, and often lean towards artistic activities. Convergent-minded children do better with straightforward question-and-answer-type tests, while divergent people prefer essays where they can use their imagination.

A typical test of convergent/divergent thinking is to ask

What you can do to help thinking

- Give lots of physical affection – touching and hugging – so that the child feels wanted and valued. Children who feel good about themselves learn better and think more.
- Keep plenty of material around for the child to learn from and with.
- Encourage your child's keenness, concentration and memory by showing delight in them.
- Show the child your own enthusiasm for ideas.
- Keep the child's learning as exciting as you can, or at least interesting. Boredom is a great turn-off.
- Don't try to push new information into a tired child. It's not your perseverance that counts, it's the child's own desire to carry on.
- Try to keep the tension level in your home as low as you can. It can act as a block on a growing mind.
- Dance together to music, to loosen up physically, before you settle down to a time of quiet thinking and talking. Little children love it.
- Lower the lighting sometimes and play different kinds of music while you talk together about ideas and matters that concern you both. Listen carefully to your child's words before you answer.
- If you feel your child is right-brain dominated, encourage the left side by playing games such as the puzzles you see in children's comics – find Farmer MacDonald's pig, for instance, hidden in a drawing of his farmyard.
- If your child seems to be left-brain dominated, encourage an appreciation of big things like the way the sky meets the earth, or give out great big pieces of paper, to paint on with a big brush.

a child what uses can be made of a brick. The converger builds houses, walls, props up shelves, etc. The diverger uses it as a paperweight, crumbles it to make cement, throws it through a window, etc. It is sometimes said that to encourage divergent thinking is only to encourage a child to be silly – which says something about the people who say this.

It's not that a child is completely one or the other kind of thinker – we need to be both to survive – but it's the dominant style we're interested in here.

WHAT ABOUT IQ?

Although the term IQ is used quite freely by parents, teachers and psychologists, controversy rages as to what it really is. Earlier this century it was thought that intelligence was fixed for life at the time of conception. But now we know that it varies a lot with circumstances, and can even change a little from day to day. Not only can each individual's score vary, but different tests produce different IQs. Of the two intelligence tests used most frequently, for example, one has an upper limit of IQ 145 and the other of IQ 170. On different tests the same child can score very differently. Sometimes tests that are designed to measure specific skills, like reading, are mistakenly used to judge IQ.

The letters IQ stand for intelligence quotient – the quotient being the result of an arithmetical division. It is a number calculated from the score a child reaches in an intelligence test. This score is called the mental age, and it is divided by the chronological age, then multiplied by a hundred to round it off, thus:

$$\frac{\text{Mental age}}{\text{Chronological age}} \times 100 = IQ$$

On average, children score around the 100 mark – 60 per cent of children score between 90 IQ and 110 IQ. A child with a score of 120 IQ or more is clearly bright; this accounts for about 10 per cent of the population. Gifted children, in the top 2 per cent, would score between 135 IQ and 170 IQ. An IQ score is always relative, giving the relationship between one child's success at certain tasks and that of all others of his own age.

But a test can only sample a child's ability at the time he takes it. It measures how well he's taken in what he's learned and how well he can reproduce it for the test, there and then. Circumstances at the time can affect the result; if he's harbouring a cold, for example, then his test result could go down.

The benefit of the intelligence test, though, is that it can act as a safety net to help children, particularly bright ones, be recognised for what they are; otherwise they may be missed and not be given a suitable education in which they can work at something like their own level. For example, a child may be mistakenly put in the bottom stream at school because he's been having trouble at home and has begun to slip back. He may lose interest there and come up with only average marks. An intelligence test would speedily alert parents and teachers to the fact that he was working well below his capacity, and they could then help him to catch up and take his rightful place in the top stream. At the very least, an intelligence test is an objective measure in a sea of opinion, but it must be used with understanding.

The very mention of IQ causes many people's hackles to rise; it may seem altogether wrong to measure children's abilities and to make decisions for their future on the basis of that measurement. People question both the standards that are being used and the moral reasons for doing it. The ability to do oneself justice in an IQ test depends a great deal on a child's opportunity to learn, such as the use of language at home, and what there is at home to play with and learn from. Without the right opportunities, some aspects of intelligence may never develop fully. Is it justifiable, then, to measure intelligence as IQ?

The following are some of the questions often asked about IQ.

Is IQ inherited?

It's difficult to say exactly how much a child's IQ is due to home background – that is, due to environment – and how much is due to heredity. Scientists can't conduct experiments with children, placing different groups in different environments to find out what happens; but nature has provided us with an ideal group for investigation, in the form of identical twins. Unlike non-identical twins – who are only as alike as ordinary brothers and sisters, but who happen to be born at the same time – identical twins are from exactly the same genetic blueprint. By looking at identical twins who have been brought up in different families we can see how the different environments have affected two children with the same genetic inheritance.

There are problems about this, though, in that the adopting families of both twins may be very similar. Adoption societies usually try to place babies with families as similar to their natural parents as possible. This has the effect of cutting down the variety of environmental differences, but, even so, it's clear that there is strong genetic inheritance of IQ. Different statistical methods, though, produce different results. Some say that 80 per cent of intelligence is inherited, which only leaves 20 per cent to be affected by the environment. The most conservative estimates say that inherited intelligence is about 30 per cent of the whole. No doubt the answer lies somewhere between the two extremes, though it is also possible that the amount of inherited IQ varies for different children.

How can environment affect intelligence?

This is a major question, which this book is aiming to answer. Circumstances (including parents' own efforts) can only affect the latent intelligence available to be developed, so it's important to know what makes a difference.

It has been found over and over again that, on average, children from the higher social classes have higher IQs than children from the lower ones. The reason for this is not that richer children are born more intelligent, but that they usually enjoy a more educationally positive upbringing. This comes from the attitudes that parents have towards their children's intellectual development, and from the standard of provision at home and school. To score highly implies a certain amount of learning, and the children who are in the best position to acquire the right kind of learning will be more likely to fulfil their learning potential – which is what the IQ test measures. Evidence from my research on above-average children showed that the two prime aspects of their lives that were most effective in raising IQ scores were their home lifestyles and their educational provision.

The question of race and its relationship to intelligence is probably the most sensitive issue in education today. Some American research, published by Professor Arthur Jensen, concluded that black children had lower IQs than white children, while other races scored in between. But this has been severely criticised on both psychological and statistical grounds; the original evidence is now virtually discredited, and even the professor has changed his mind somewhat. As if to underline this point, Japanese children are seen to be gaining in IQ points at a greater rate than most other groups. This may be due to the pressure of their educational experience, which stresses the acquisition of information and could push their scores up, as well as to their improved nutrition.

The IQ test does not measure creative endeavour. Where children are judged individually, regardless of race, each is then free to find their own limitations and strengths through the experience of their own activities.

Can IQ predict success?

IQ certainly can predict some kinds of success, such as school and university achievement, extremely well – but then so does a child's social background, because it tends to be linked with IQ. However the possession of a high IQ alone is not enough to predict success at anything else. The proportion of high-IQ people in the population can easily be calculated, and only some of them could be called successful in worldly terms, while, on the other hand, many people with lower IQs are extremely successful.

Personality and outlook are just as important for success as IQ. In fact, if a child is aiming to be a self-made millionaire then a highly developed IQ, which could lead to much time being spent at a university, and thought processes being trained to criticise rather than construct, can be a positive hindrance.

Do boys and girls have different IQs?

It isn't possible to say that one sex is more intelligent than the other, but there is evidence for a greater range of intelligence among boys, i.e. a boy has a greater chance than a girl of being either stupid or gifted. But even after nearly a century of practice the measurement of intelligence is still so unsure that there may be perfectly good social reasons for these differences, only some of which are known at present. For example, it is known that mentally subnormal boys are far more likely to be institutionalised than girls, possibly because it is more acceptable to have such girls about the house. It may be that social reasons are responsible for the relative lack of gifted girls who come to be noticed; their drive to achieve is possibly deflected into other behaviour that is considered more acceptable for them.

The main problem with an IQ score is that the figure stands for a whole collection of abilities. It's a bit like saying that your personality is PQ 124 – not really very informative. In fact the newest intelligence scales are giving up the idea of a single number IQ, and presenting their results as a profile of abilities. Since boys and girls have different rates and types of intellectual development, their results in tests must be seen in relation to the age at which they are measured. The future adult intelligence of girls, for instance, can be predicted when they are between three and six years old, but that of boys has to wait until they are between six and ten. During this later period of development, almost twice as many boys as girls show increases in IQ. In addition, girls are generally better with language and boys with numbers, so that if a test is made up with a bias towards either of these abilities, the one sex scores more highly. Psychological researchers are still hard at work trying to sort out the influences of heredity and environment in these sex differences, as well as all the other controversies about IQ.

What is the future for intelligence testing?

There are dozens of new ideas coming out of the psychology laboratories about how to measure intelligence. Future test-takers, for example may be:

- Listening to clicks in earphones or watching flashing lights, while electrodes taped to their temples send brain responses to be analysed by a computer.
- Held (as babies) to watch toy cars knocking dolls over, while having their heartbeats measured.
- Tracing a stencil.
- Describing their daily lives.
- Organising dots.
- Deciding at three years old how they would behave if they were in a game that needed three children and only two wanted to play.
- Pressing buttons as fast as they can.

Researchers in Russia, where the concept of IQ has never been popular, are aiming to measure learning potential. This approach involves giving children unfamiliar problems and measuring the number of 'prompts' or the amount of coaching they need before they can solve the problems. In the west an attempt is being made to find out the different steps in the reasoning processes, though it sometimes seems as though we know more and more about less and less.

Can parents raise a child's IQ?

With the knowledge we already have it is possible to raise the IQ of a child by as much as 20 points, particularly if he has been culturally deprived, and it may be possible to

What you can do about IQ

- Do your best to provide children with toys, drawing paper, musical instruments – anything that they can use to practise their intellectual and artistic skills – and be as generous as possible. Buy wallpaper lining paper, for example, rather than drawing paper, so that a child can scribble without you feeling that she's just wasting money. Don't stint on giving her things to play and work with.

- Make your own lives challenging and full, so far as possible. It's important for children to see their parents making good use of their intelligence . Let the children join in with your activities where you can – sit down and listen to music sessions together, for example. Any music will do, it's the lively minded listening that's important.

- Try to be realistic about your child's abilities. Although high expectations can work wonders, if they're too high it can cause damage. When a child can't reach the goal you've set because it's too high, her feelings of self-worth can slump with her failure.

- Check constantly to see that your child isn't being organised into rigid ways of thinking that are said to be appropriate for her or his sex, but which may, in fact, be quite inappropriate for the individual concerned.

- Think positively and give lots of praise – where it is merited – so that you build up an atmosphere of trust and acceptance in the home. This gives the child the psychological freedom to explore new ideas and knowledge, without the fear of being put down by sarcasm or sharp correction.

increase this advantage in the future. Suggestions on how this is done are given throughout this book.

We also know of some brakes on IQ development within a child's physical environment. For example, it is now clear that lead pollution from car exhausts and industrial waste does lower a child's developing intelligence. Non-stop noise – even loud music – played within a baby's earshot can actually be harmful to her IQ development because it interferes with her ability to choose what to listen to.

The earliest IQ development occurs in a parent's natural 'conversations' with the baby. The parent often imitates the baby's sounds, waits for a response from the baby, and then imitates that. After a while the parent may begin to introduce new sounds and words – 'Now I'm going to tickle your tummy.' It's the baby's response that is important, and the changes this brings about in her mind. 'Conversation' also helps babies to develop their communication by facial expressions, and then a sense of trust builds up. To say that children should be seen but not heard would be to limit their intellectual growth; fortunately, it never happens in reality.

The sooner parents begin to foster IQ in a baby's life, the more effective they are likely to be, though development never stops at any age; it's the rate of development that changes, and the swiftest is from birth to age two. The longer you wait after that, the harder it is. There are also specially sensitive periods in a child's life when learning takes on a growth spurt. One of these periods appears to end at about age four, and another takes place between the ages of four and eight. The age at which children start school, between four and five, is possibly an age at which there is a lower rate of mental growth.

The key problem for parents is in finding circumstances that are sufficiently lively and stimulating for a child, yet not too demanding at his particular point of development. If it's too easy, learning becomes stale; too hard, and it's distressing. But a really good match of ability and challenge brings about such pleasure and increased desire for learning in the child that he will keep going under his own steam, and there should be no need to worry about pushing. Intelligence grows from the child's own attempts to cope with his circumstances – from his experiences in dealing with things and people around him, and seeing what happens. Providing for this is just part of the art of parenting.

6
THE DELIGHT
OF DISCOVERY

It's the extra urge to find things out and make things of his own that puts a bright child a cut above the rest. The searching creative child knows that there are many things to be discovered, sorted out and improved on; that's why he works so earnestly at them. Being bright suggests more than an ability to copy, though there's a lot of skill in that too.

First-hand experience is needed to build up impressions and ideas, not just from touching and seeing, but also from rubbing up against another interested mind. The apparently 'silly' ideas and 'stupid' questions of early childhood are, in fact, a form of exploration and testing that should not just be irritably dismissed – at least not most of them.

ENCOURAGING DISCOVERY

The delight of discovery begins at birth – all babies know it. But those who are fortunate enough to keep it with them, maybe for life, have a constant yearning to learn, to invent problems and to solve them. Life can be continuously creative and satisfying for children if they get off to the right start. It's no use waiting for school to provide the inspiration for this because it may never happen there, and anyway it's getting a bit late by then – ways of exploring learning are formed at home.

Toys are important to children's learning, but especially when they can create with them – there is no obligation to follow the makers' instructions. A child may find that building wooden jigsaw pieces into a tower satisfies her more than putting them in the spaces provided. John and Elizabeth Newson describe more toys than you can imagine in their book *Toys and Playthings*, and offer lots of ideas to parents.

Of course, children often rate adult activities higher than the toys they're given to play with. Let them become involved with what you are doing about the house, 'working' with you, knocking in nails, cooking or gardening. Try to talk about these things as you do them, connecting up the activities with ideas and then carefully going back over what you've done together.

Children do not need to be pushed to explore; all toddlers are proof of that. But they do need plenty of opportunities for experience, and the wider the variety, the broader the base they will have on which to build their creative awareness. Where variety is difficult to come by naturally, as in a tiny tenth-floor apartment, parents have to make an even greater effort to provide it. Television can help. For example, the American television series *Sesame Street*, and many European children's programmes, are specially designed for this purpose. Then there is the local library service; it's free and particularly useful for toddlers. There are certain to be plenty of lovely picture books and you may find pre-school reading sessions held there. You could take your toddler to art galleries and museums too, but be sure to keep the outings fun and not too long; trailing wearily round room after room of an exhibition with eager parents is more tiring than inspiring.

It is possible to teach children to use their senses to the full. If they are only aware of part of the world they live in, they will have that much less choice of material to grow with and to create from. Being creative, in however small a way, is demanding, and needs time for ideas and products to be developed. Painting on a wet afternoon is fine, but it rather loses its pleasure and satisfaction if a child is constantly being interrupted to do this and that, and then finally told to put it all away before he feels it is properly finished. Sometimes, if a creative child is really involved in a piece of work, he may have to go back to it many times over a period of weeks. Also, although there is excitement in discovery, there may also be despair in failure to produce just what he wants, and when parents hear that heartfelt cry 'I can't do it', they should give their encouragement and interest to see the child through.

In fact, other people's appreciation is a very powerful force on creativity. Slowed-down videos have been very informative on this. For example, a toddler who is painting on a big sheet of paper with a big brush on a table is watched by her mother. She watches her mother carefully out of the corner of her eye, and moves according to how she 'reads' her mother's responses and interest in her activity. Even very small children do not dab paint on to paper at random. They choose their design, whether straight lines or curved ones (however scribbled it may look to others), and choose the colours (even before they can name them). But they may change their minds and choose to do something else if they get a non-intentional signal from mother.

A child's treasured works should be displayed where everyone can admire them, and not just confined to the child's bedroom or put on one side out of the way. My research has shown that children whose pictures make it to the living room wall, especially framed, become more interested in art and so usually do better at it. Any creative activity is a form of self-expression, and what a child makes for herself is more important to her than any objectively judged level of achievement. If parents and others are obviously pleased by the result, the child's own satisfaction will be many times greater.

Creative activity is so often considered only as play, when it is really an important part of all learning. In fact, the enjoyment which most children find nowadays in their school work is largely due to its new creative aspect. Learning through doing is not only more fun, but more easily remembered and put to use. The child from an open-minded yet ordered home will probably do better at school than one from a more conforming and rigid background.

There are many practical ways of helping a child to express himself creatively, although the most obvious is painting. If a parent makes sure that child, floor and working surfaces are protected from the paint, this will give the psychological go-ahead. Of course, a child must learn to use his tools – too wet a brush, or paper that's too thin will impede the creative flow. Water for the paint must be changed often, and a good supply of tissues should be to hand for wiping brushes. But remember that your way of seeing is not his – a purple tree is every bit as good as a green one.

Children are sometimes happier making three-dimensional things. Masses of cardboard and sticky tape can make complicated dwellings, and even towns. Plasticine carved with a blunt knife can produce most impressive results, whilst older primary school children can be taught to use a sharper knife and carve – always cutting away from themselves – in balsa wood or soap. Ready-bought modelling sets are not always value for money, and can take away the thrill of having made something all by themselves, though they do teach precision. Little children have great fun with glue and round-ended scissors, cutting up bits of cloth and wallpaper, which they can stick on cardboard to make a picture. Some like making human figures and some prefer patterns. The design can either be drawn out first, or made up as they go along.

Most primary schools now provide creative opportunities, but if you happen to live in the area of one which doesn't, you may have to make up for it at home. A school which only dishes up the three Rs, with a sprinkling of community singing and crayoning, isn't providing a balanced education. It is also likely to mean that the vital enthusiasm and spirit of which the children are capable either dies away or is kept for out-of-school interests. See what books your local library has on creative work at home. Don't be put off by pictures in them of children's drawings which always seem outstandingly better than the efforts in your own home; there is something about the printed page that gives glamour to even the simplest scribble.

Exceptionally creative children can be very deprived in an old-fashioned school. Because such a child is often the most lively in the class, she may be considered a nuisance by teachers. But the creative child has something special to offer the world; she is the only one who questions what has always been accepted. She is likely to be both sensitive to others and highly critical of herself, as well as having a sense of humour and fun.

Parents direct their children in two ways. The first of these is imperative: 'Be quiet, because I say so.' The second is instructive: 'Be quiet, so you can hear the birds singing.' To help your child towards an adventurous mind you should rarely use the imperative, and in fact it is not often needed. The instructive approach is far better, as it helps the child towards thinking things through for himself, which is the very foundation of creative thinking.

There is evidence to show that parents who put strict limits on their children's freedom of action, with a constant stream of 'Don'ts', also restrict their curiosity and urge for independent thinking. What may happen as they get older is that instead of being well behaved and obedient, they can become very rebellious, distressed and distressing. 'Don't touch' is probably a parent's most frequently used admonition, and its overuse can shut a child's windows on the world; the best plan is to put the crystal glasses out of a child's reach until she's older. The more creative thinkers come from homes that are less bound by concern for conventional academic success, and where the children are given a wide choice of friends and activities.

To be imaginative and creative a child doesn't have to be highly intelligent; great artists, for example, are not specially known for their brilliant intellects. It's only possible to say that, whereas a high intelligence does not guarantee high creativity, a low one certainly works against it.

However, it must be remembered that discovery on its own isn't very useful; it has to be tied up to what a child knows already and then judged by him for what it's worth. It works like a revolving kaleidoscope – you rummage through what you know and form new patterns, and, from those, you can take the creative leap to new ideas. Clever little Henry did just that sort of jump when he was three years old; he couldn't write, but he could form numbers, so when he wanted to make a note of his birthday he put 22 on his birthday cards. 'It was Tuesday', he explained, so that's why he wrote the pair of 2s.

BRAINSTORMING

Parents can teach children to think creatively; the most successful methods use the child's intelligence and feelings together. Mental exercise is the key. When a big business is short of ideas, its chief directors get together for a day or two for a brainstorming session. What they're doing is bombarding their brains with each other's experiences and activities. The ensuing kaleidoscope triggers off further connections of ideas and brings about new ones. It is also a bringing together of everyone's thinking styles, so that right and left brainers, convergent and divergent thinkers, can all stimulate each other's thinking. The essential ground rule is never be negative, accept ideas as they flow, without a single 'Yes, but ...'.

The first step in teaching a child (or adult) to think creatively is to improve her awareness. You can present a problem to a child which is just within her capacity to have a stab at solving. Some questions you could put, for example, would be:

- For a three year old: 'What can you do with a piece of paper?'
- For a five year old: 'What would happen if everyone doubled in height?'
- For a ten year old: 'What do we need to do to feed the world's people?'

Here are some real mind-teasers from an American educational system called syntectics:

- The sky darkening before a storm is like what in the animal world? Why?
- How is a metal base spring like hope?
- An iceberg is like a big idea because ...?
- If a lake were a table, what would the boats be?

You could try a small-scale creativity brainstorming session, starting with some of these questions, or others like them, that have no obvious answers. The idea is to stretch the child's imagination as far as possible.

You can have a session with one child, but it's more fun with a few. Start by trying to think around possible answers to the questions, making sure that the child feels free to use his imagination. No judgment is allowed; there is no right or wrong response. That is a simple rule, and it helps encourage real free choice in a protected atmosphere, but it can be amazingly difficult. Usually, children begin by testing the rule – they can't believe in their good fortune at being free. But if you stick to it, they soon come to recognise and respect their own and others' ideas. Exercising the mind in these conditions enhances the child's feelings of self-worth and personal power. It is in the climate of trust, so essential to creative thought, that he can go ahead with intellectual risk-taking. Keep up the brainstorming at as swift a pace as the situation will allow, letting imagination strike out more and more widely, questioning and making suggestions, again alternately. Children usually love the thrill of the mental chase.

The result of this sort of exercise should be to help children use more and different kinds of ideas in making decisions. But it needs some sensitivity and control by parents. In the same way as you know when children are becoming overtired and in need of sleep, then you will feel when they are getting too excited, and you can act to stop the session before they become exhausted and overwhelmed. Sometimes the participants are overcome by giggles, which is OK from time to time, but that needs control too, or the exercise loses its point. If there is the slightest hint of fatigue, then carefully bring the session to a halt, using your parental skills. At the end, the children should feel on top of the world.

The Bulgarians have a system called suggestology, which works on the principle of pleasure in learning. First of all the child relaxes her mind, but stays ready for action. Then she and her parents or teacher suggest some understanding of how different ideas and things can be seen together. For example, you could relax with your child and let ideas about wheels, axles, gravity and weight float about in your minds. They may then bump about, setting each other off, and cling together in new ways. It's rather like brainstorming, but without the tension, and you could end up designing a waggon to the moon.

AWAY INTO FANTASY

Creative thinking is normally tied up with feelings and needs, desires and fears; daydreaming is an example of this kind of thought. A little girl playing with her dolls is exploring and sorting out her feelings about family life; the experience is helping her come to terms with her own need for love and care, and she's learning to handle her fantasies at the same time. Great artists, writers and scientists use these childlike mental explorations to help them in their work. Though they can never regain the genuine innocence of childhood, creative people have to be open to fantasy and less hampered by judgments of right and wrong than most of us. This enables them to produce original ideas, which then have to be worked out in detail using adult skills. This is how it seems to work.

- Preparation. This is the hard work, where the creative person gets to know all he can in his field of endeavour, such as what work has been done previously in it, what techniques are available, etc. This is the essential basis for creative thinking.
- Unconscious thinking. The person now puts all his work aside, shoves everything to the back of his mind and gets on with something else. It's a sort of fermentation process, which can go on for minutes or years.
- Inspiration. An idea can come at any time, but is most likely while drifting off to sleep or waking up. It's very exciting when something is on the way, even if it is only the germ of an idea.
- Working it out. The process of going back to the drawing board with the new inspiration, logically checking it and following ideas through, is a vital part of making the creative product. This is where real skill and expertise show themselves.

Some creative works can take a very long time; the composer Wagner worked on The Ring cycle of operas for over 26 years. Edison is often quoted as having said that genius is 1 per cent inspiration and 99 per cent perspiration.

The future
Bright aware children are often very concerned for the future of 'spaceship earth'. They are attracted by unknown possibilities and feel challenged to take part in solving problems that have yet to appear. The thought processes needed for sensing and solving future problems are

associated with a high level of ability, and it is the children who are most concerned about the future in many avenues of life – cultural, scientific, political and educational – who are our most promising natural resource. So it is important to involve bright children in the problems of the world, and not only those of their own community. Unfortunately, much of what is taught in schools, especially to the most intelligent pupils, is concerned with doggedly acquiring and reproducing information, and this can blunt any child's natural curiosity and desire for change. If a child is limited in his thinking to what's already known, then how is he going to make decisions about what's not yet known?

INDEPENDENCE AND CONFORMITY

Creative children are particularly independent, which may even be seen in their relationships with their families. They usually come from homes where they are given a lot of encouragement in what they want to do. If a child is truly absorbed in finding out about things, encourage her. There's a noticeable difference between commitment and obstinacy, which parents are usually able to judge. The interests that children have are the best signs of how they're going to grow up. Do they like to make things or to play music, or do they read more than their schoolmates? Even though children's interests change, they usually develop along a recognisable theme. It's worth writing in your diary what interests your child shows and how intense she is about them. If you don't know already, it will give an idea of her real interests and some clues as to how she might make her future.

So much of the natural creative spirit that every baby is born with seems to get squashed out of existence by social pressure to conform. A little boy, for example, may be told that he should not be indoors working on his model aeroplane, but outdoors, kicking a ball with the other boys. Why? Is it always healthier? Or a little girl may be discouraged from playing with a toy car or engine because her parents feel strongly that this is not suitable for a

What you can do to help discovery

- If at all possible, see that the child has enough time and space to be alone with peace of mind, so that she can practise and explore knowledge in a psychologically safe secure setting.
- A child has to have the right working materials. For example, Yehudi Menuhin couldn't have been a violinist had his parents not bought him a tiny violin. Make sure there's a generous supply of paper and paints around, and egg-boxes and other containers to glue together to make models. Teach children how to work with the minimum of mess – and to clear up when they're finished. But always give them a place to do it in where mess doesn't matter.
- Neither interfere constantly, nor expect immediate results. A painting a day may not be the best way.
- Give a lot of support and encouragement. Creativity is anxiety-producing; the most creative people are those who can best tolerate anxiety.
- Be totally accepting of the child's need for privacy and make-believe, and don't ever let sarcasm creep into your voice, even if you think it's only a joke.
- Show by your own lifestyle that discovery is a pleasure. Keep your own interests alive and share them with your child. You could, for example, learn about your home district together.
- Keep your directions positive; 'Do' works better than 'Don't'.
- Encourage children to use their playthings in new ways. Even babies do it. Instead of rattling their rattles, for example, they learn all too quickly to throw them to the ground for the fun of watching you pick them up.

daughter, that she would lose some femininity by it.

Lively minded creative children need to have the confidence and the will to step out of line sometimes. The sort of child who thinks differently from her friends is likely to have an independent nature and be sure of herself. She needs to have the mental freedom to be able to free herself at times from what is usually considered 'right' or 'wrong' ways of thinking and doing, so that she can work with her own sense of values, along with an understanding of the more usual ways.

If you think you might have such a child in your family, remember that there is a difference between bad behaviour and independence, just as there is between a child who is happier doing things on his own and one who is alone because no one wants to play with him. A tolerant child is not the same as one who cannot make up his mind about anything. Finally, there is a real difference between the 'product' that is merely cute and one that is truly creative and original. If you're not sure which you're faced with, get whatever expert advice you can. Real creativity shouldn't be missed – for the child's sake and for the benefit of everybody else.

The greatest enemy to imaginative thinking and change is conformity. Clever children need exercise for their growing and maturing capacities, so that they can have control and confidence in what they can do. It gives them the security to find new knowledge and approach new problems through sharing, rather than by hugging facts to themselves in narrow short-sighted competition.

7 PREPARING FOR SCHOOL

It's the little everyday things that can make all the difference to your happiness and success in bringing up a bright child who is ready to get the best out of school. A sensible move is to try to get your house organised right from the beginning so that it's a lived in but efficient place for learning, leaving you with the greatest possible amount of time to devote to your child. Here are some ideas that you can adapt to your own circumstances.

PLAY

There is something about the way a very bright child enjoys learning that can give parents the impression that playing is, for them, a waste of time. A bright child with his knowing ways can even seem like a miniature adult. But the richness of life as a child is in play, and stepping up the school-type work takes it away. It's a basic rule of child development that even the most sophisticated and mature child still needs to play, even if they need encouragement to do it.

The value of play is not only in the amusement and relaxation it gives a child, but also for the learning it provides – both emotional and intellectual. Emotionally, even a toddler can play out aspects of his life that he doesn't quite understand, so that he becomes more familiar with what's going on and finds it easier to live with. Intellectually, play lets a child take in new information and manipulate it to fit in with what he knows already. Through play, a child can practise, improve his thinking and develop his creativity. Play with other children is a very valuable means of learning social and communication skills, especially for children who have a tendency to be solitary.

As well as everyday play, which children choose to enjoy, parents can make suggestions for play. Playgroups and nursery schools direct play with sand and water, and in the group activities. Here are a few ideas for parents at home, which offer bright children some mental exercise:

- Have your three year old imagine she's a robot. Then let her work out what effect this would have on the world if it were really true. Encourage her to think about how robots would change the way we live. Together you can broaden this idea over time to consider all sorts of imaginary technical inventions.
- Next time your toddler piles up his blocks into a tall and shaky tower, talk to him about it. See if he can tell you what would happen if he put a bigger block on top, or a smaller one. Then get him to try out his 'hypothesis', using the smaller block first. Perhaps, by some judicious questions and suggestions, you could work his mind round to the idea that some blocks can

act to support the tower (buttresses). This sort of play helps to teach technical problem-solving skills.

- A bright four year old can have a lot of fun thinking up her own games, rather than just following the rules of those she knows already. Suggest to her that she makes up a game, with her own rules, using something she's interested in – like a set of her favourite toy animals. Then try out the game with the other children she plays with.

Helping children play

Homes where little children are growing and learning are usually a mess. There are paints and toys, bits of paper, cushions, and all sorts of things that they need for daily living, but which, overall, don't do much for the decor. Take it easy, though; it's like that for everyone who hasn't got a nanny to supervise the nursery. It's very likely that this is the way it's going to be for some years, so don't make constant efforts to keep the place in perfect order. It only frays everyone's nerves and can slow up the children's learning when, for example, they can't cut up pieces of paper without a scolding. If you would like a nice area to be alone in or for entertaining your friends – and who doesn't – then make a space just for parents. If you have a separate living room, it could be forbidden to unaccompanied children.

An educationally stimulating home has pictures on the walls, as well as ornaments and things to handle. Music is also important; not just the background muzak interspersed with chatter that comes over the radio for hours, but real sit-down pay-attention bursts of something you all enjoy. A sense of rhythm helps children to speak early and to develop in a more balanced way.

When your child is old enough to draw, make sure his efforts go up on the wall – and in important places, too, not just in the kitchen. Mount them simply, as many primary schools do, on thick cardboard with a bold felt tip line ruled around, so that they're shown to their best advantage.

You'll all get a lot of pleasure and pride from looking at them. You can attach them with something like Blu-Tak, and the mounts can be used again. Change them from time to time so that he is encouraged to do more; it shows your respect and appreciation of his efforts. And if he hasn't got to that stage yet, then stick posters or pictures of your own up.

All children should have a place for their own books, right from the start. It doesn't have to be a smart bookcase, as long as it is somewhere the child knows she can go and find something to read. Either visit the library or buy her a new book from time to time, especially if you think she's ready to move on with her reading. Each child in the family should have her own supply of books which are hers alone so that she can learn to care for them and use them in her own way. The book area should be attractive and the books stored not too close together, so that little fingers can get hold of them easily.

For the same reasons it's better for children to have a special place for their toys. It should be big and reachable enough to make a child's clearing-up job easy, so that the mess can be kept to a reasonable level. If he has to put things carefully one on top of another in his cupboard, he'll be less inclined to take that trouble, and will either ignore his instructions or jumble things in anyhow and maybe break them.

Keep messy and water play strictly to the kitchen and bathroom; your child can then have a great time splashing and learning about the properties of water, without fear of a telling-off. If you let him trail around the house with paints, you'll all suffer from the stains and their consequences.

The material that children use for learning is important, and there should be plenty of it. You will need lots of sharpened pencils, felt-tip pens, paints, brushes and paper. Wallpaper lining paper is handy at first, then older children can move on to drawing paper bought in bulk. Children need scissors and paste; nowadays paste comes in solid form, so there needn't be quite the sticky mess there always was when my own children were small. Be lavish but not profligate with materials. It's part of their learning process that children should appreciate value.

Junk has its uses, as every parent and primary school teacher knows. Egg boxes, toilet roll holders, jam jars and so on are the stock-in-trade of the learning child, the basis of thousands of imaginative models. Add to that beans, seeds, shells, fir cones, wrapping paper, cloth, etc. – the supply is endless, and virtually free. Keep a special overall to hand for a child to work in, such as an old shirt, and be sure his wet-work overall is waterproof.

Children have to clear up. Be firm, give them warnings and plenty of time, but you must supervise. Even a two year old can make a good job of it, with a little help from mummy or daddy. Encourage children to help each other so that it doesn't matter who made what mess; otherwise, you can spend a good deal of time in negative argument. If there's a real reluctance, start by handing out simple tasks, such as 'Peter, please put your pencils in this box so that I can put it in the cupboard.' Don't nag, be specific, and give lots of praise where it's due.

NURSERY SCHOOL

All the good preparation that parents put into their children's early lives really goes to work when the child comes under the care of a teacher. For many children this can start from about the age of two, when they may begin with a few hours a week at nursery school.

Though some parents do not like the idea of very little children being away from their homes regularly, there is a lot of evidence to show that children who do go to nursery school settle down more quickly and get on better at 'proper' school. My own four children all went to a nursery school, starting in their third year. It seemed to me, as a mother, that they were all very happy there, and none of them had problems in transferring on.

When a child is about three, he begins to need a bit of social life. His nearest and dearest, on whom he has been dependent for so long, somehow do not quite fill his life completely any more, and parents may well need a break too. One way of helping a child's social life along, now and in the future, is to give him the company of others of his own age. It helps a little child to get a sense of identity and encourages his unfolding individuality.

The exclusive parent–child relationship, which has endured all his life so far, is not 'natural' in many societies – it only happens in the western world. All over Africa and Asia, for instance, parents have children playing with other children as soon as they can stagger about. There's no convincing psychological or anthropological evidence to suggest that our style of parenting is instinctive or even natural. So much of the way we adults act as parents is the way we have learned to behave; it is part of the way in which cultural values are passed on to the next generation.

Children, though, need more than love and care from their parents; for a balanced development they need to be with others of their own age. It has long been known to parents that toddlers can take comfort from being with other children, and bright children like to be with older children too. Some recent research in California, which looked at babies of only nine months, showed that even at their age, the group of babies that spent time with others got to know them and became friends, in their limited way. This could be seen in their responses, the 'friends' being different with each other compared with the babies who had just met.

In a famous experiment the American Professor Harry Harlow showed that monkeys raised without their mothers did not grow up to lead the normal social lives of monkeys, and became isolates. However, when he put another motherless group in with their age-mates, for as little as 20 minutes a day, their social, emotional and intellectual development improved. The age-mates had provided much of the social learning. Studies with human toddlers have shown that, particularly where the use of language in the home is poor, other children in a nursery can be a valuable source of language and thinking skills. But this does not apply to all children, all the time. A child's fullest language capacities are still best developed from talk at home, which can be richer and more finely tuned than most of the interactions at nursery school.

A major American follow-up study on pre-school education, by the High Scope Education Foundation in Michigan, has shown how valuable teaching very little children can be in a poor community. Looking at poor black children, they found that by the age of 19 those who had gone to nursery school were more likely to have finished high school and almost twice as likely to have found jobs than those who had not. As a group, they were also less likely to commit crimes, and the girls had fewer teenage pregnancies. How much better it would be if all children were to have the option of taking nursery education.

Unfortunately, though, in the UK there never seem to be enough nursery places for all the parents who would like their children to make use of them; this can even be the case in other countries where they pride themselves on their state provision of nursery education, such as in eastern Europe. An alternative in this country is to make use of a private nursery school; however, although such a school may be excellent, it may be too expensive for many families. Other nursery schools may have opening hours that make it difficult for working parents to leave their children there. The answer must be to extend nursery school hours, which could be done for comparatively little money, as in France; nurseries could, for example, be housed in school classrooms after school.

Pre-school playgroups

In 1961 a nursery school teacher in Britain, Belle Tutaev, wrote to a newspaper calling for more government sponsored nursery facilities. But she also suggested an alternative – that parents start their own. She was quickly flooded with replies from mothers eager to start, and within a few years the nationwide Pre-school Playgroups Association was formed. Although Britain is still at the bottom of the European league table for nursery provision, as only about a fifth of all our children have access to free nurseries, the Pre-school Playgroups Association now has about 15,000 member groups.

The benefits to both mother and child are considerable. For the children, extended language learning through verse and song is only part of the greater freedom to play imaginatively and to learn to socialise. For the parents, such as working mothers, the playgroups provide safe care for little ones, often with trained staff. Parents of playgroupers are also more likely to become more deeply involved in their children's future education, joining parent–teacher associations and school governing bodies.

The one stipulation with playgroups, however, is that parents are usually expected to take their share of responsibility for the group, which may be difficult to fit in with a work schedule. It's important to choose the

---

What to look for in a nursery school

- Is the atmosphere lively, and are the children's educational experiences stimulating and encouraging?
- Are the staff well trained, and do they stay?
- Is the nursery well organised, or is there little rationale in the activities chosen?
- Is there a warm and loving atmosphere?
- Is the atmosphere designed to make children feel at ease and happy? A nursery is not a copy of home, but it can have an intimate feeling by, for example, having the children in little groups for special play or listening to a story. It should be like a child's second home.
- Do the staff and children seem to get on together, or is there a feeling that the children have to do as they're told, or else? A punitive atmosphere can make children unhappy and set up anti-education feelings in them for life.

playgroup that suits you best, to shop around for one in which both the child and the parent feel comfortable.

For working parents in areas without either playgroups or nurseries, the only options are often the services of grandparents willing to help out, or a paid pre-school childminder, who may or may not be registered. Although possibly quite acceptable as minders, an untrained childminder is no substitute for a nursery teacher in terms of early education. Quite a number of recent surveys into childminding have provided reason for some concern. For example, Professor Jerome Bruner, the American educationalist, found from his Oxford survey that childminding 'is a risky form of care even with sympathetic and kindly, conventionally competent child minders'. Obviously, though, every childminder should be judged on their own merits. Bruner suggested that childminders would be most suitably employed working alongside trained child-care-givers; they could be used as extras in nursery schools, or as a timely help between the close of school and parents finishing work.

All pre-school education, whether playgroup or nursery school, is an extension of, not a substitute for, the private family world in which children grow best. The progression from home to pre-school should be as smooth and easy as possible. Parents should never feel that they are giving over control of their child's early education to a nursery school teacher. The family is still all important. For all that he is away for a few hours a day, the child is still a member of his family and his parents are still by far the most influential people he knows.

DAUGHTERS

The poet who wrote 'Be good, sweet maid, and let who will be clever' summed up some attitudes towards bright girls – attitudes that are still around today. Though baby girls and boys do not start off with different aspirations, somehow the messages of what each should aim for seem to get through to them. Many surveys have shown that, in general, girls are less keen to succeed in worldly terms than their brothers. They are also more likely to value a future occupation for the satisfaction it would bring them, rather than for its possible rewards of money or status.

These expectations take shape as girls grow and learn, and can eventually result in a poorer level of intellectual activity than they are capable of reaching. Boys often seem to have more confidence in their native ability than girls, so that girls are more modest about their abilities and achievements, even when their results are exactly the same. As a result, they tend to attribute their school success to hard work, whereas boys say it's because they themselves are clever.

In America, a nationwide survey has found that many girls in mixed schools actually lower their goals, so that the boys will like them more. Even those girls who did come top of the class seemed to see it as some sort of 'mistake'. In fact, the best chance of educational success a girl has is in an all-girls school. But doing well in particular subjects seems to vary from place to place. In Japan and Russia, for instance, where women's employment patterns are different, girls do relatively much better in science and maths than they do in other countries.

Bright girls are very aware of what is expected of their sex. Highly intelligent girls can have particular problems due to conflicts between achieving and being feminine. So, when she reaches the age of 11 or 12, it may seem easier for a girl to drop one of these supposedly conflicting aims. This lack of balance shows when she either becomes overly concerned with traditional feminine things, like making herself pretty, and does less than her best at school; or she may work extremely hard at school, setting very high standards for herself and seeming to despair if she does not always reach them. Clever girls can be very thin-skinned and over-react to this vulnerability by being bossy and domineering, sometimes at the expense of their qualities of imagination and creativity. So girls who do well at school may sometimes seem ruthlessly ambitious or insensitive. But this can be really quite an untrue picture; inside, they

What you can do for your daughter

- Ask her how hard she finds her lessons. If she says they're easy, then she's probably intellectually under-exercised. Bright girls need challenges, and are less likely to seek it out for themselves than boys.
- Talk to her teacher if you think your daughter is only 'treading water' at school. The teacher will probably be glad you brought the situation to her notice, and together you can work out some way of getting your daughter to operate at her true level.
- Treat your daughter in a way that respects her intelligence. Don't baby her, or underestimate her abilities. Try not to make too many assumptions. Let your son help with the ironing, for example, while your daughter changes the light bulb.
- Help your daughter to explore her feelings about being clever and being a girl. Talk about school, what it means to her and how she expects to get on there and afterwards. Help her find her true interests, so that she can make the best career decisions when the time comes. It's never too early, since girls begin to get pushed in the directions considered appropriate to their sex from the time they're born.
- Show your daughter successful women at work; if appropriate, her mother might be the best example. Point out how women can be doctors, not only nurses, and that maybe one day she'll be the first woman in her own field.
- Be sure your encouragement for your daughter is real and that there aren't some secret hopes in your heart that one day she'll 'settle down' and make motherhood her only career. Many girls receive confusing messages, when parents say 'Be a lawyer' with their mouths but 'Be a housewife' with their tone.

can be impatient and hungry for reassurance about everything, especially their femininity. Give them lots of praise, even (or specially) when they seem too big for their boots.

On the other hand, there are many more nice bright girls who sit quietly through lessons at school, demanding nothing and doing only as well as they're expected to. If parents or teachers give them more difficult work, they rise to the occasion, showing that the ability is there, but it often isn't recognised, since these girls don't claim enough attention for themselves. What tends to happen is that teachers see the boys as cleverer, and give them the extra attention, which brings them on further. Those who demand more are more likely to be spotted; parents should therefore watch out for this in their well-behaved daughters.

GOOD STUDY METHODS

Learning how to learn begins when a child is tiny, yet it can affect the way she will tackle any task throughout her life. This is well under way when she finds out that skill and patience are more likely to get her shaped block through the slot in the toy 'post box' than banging it down angrily; and she'll use that understanding again. Later on she may find that she has better friendships if she doesn't grab toys from her playmates' hands at nursery school. Soon she will learn how to get the teacher's attention by asking for it in just the right way – children who are too shy are sometimes left alone by the teacher and so can miss some vital teaching, whereas those who are too demanding may be pushed aside in irritation at their behaviour.

In writing about study methods here, I'm concerned with a child's growing mastery of his own learning, but these acquired skills are also very useful for older children and adults. Though you are probably reading this book to find out more about bright children, perhaps it may offer a personal bonus.

Having the right approach to their work from their first

days at school can make a big difference in future tests and exams. Good study habits formed at home and at school also continue to be of great value as youngsters move on from school to higher education and adult life. It seems extraordinary to me that schools don't usually teach study methods, leaving most children to devise their own systems. Yet the basis of good study is easily remembered by a bright child, and gives great satisfaction in practice. Here are some ideas that can be useful throughout childhood.

The will to study

The question of motivation is foremost here, and problems with it are not uncommon (see Chapter 9). Children, especially bright ones, can become devoted to just a few aspects of their interests – such as science and not the arts – at school, so that they won't sit down and learn history as they're supposed to. Find out why this is so; talk about it with the child. Sometimes a subject can be dropped with little harm done, but it may need to be gone through, even mechanically, just to provide a reasonably wide educational base. A child should understand why he is expected to do this particular work, though there has to be something in it for him too, not just for parents or for the sake of school routine. Even small children can understand that learning about other people (geography and history) helps them to learn about the world so that they can cope with their own lives a little better, that English helps them to communicate, and that being able to add up correctly means that they pay the correct price for something.

Organisation

Parents often work on the assumption that teachers are helping children to develop home study skills in the homework they set, but this is rarely true. Lively minded children may want to work around a subject or follow their own interests, and any investigation is more effective when it is properly organised. Firstly, it is usually best to take an overall view of what is to be done, whether project or exam revision. The child should learn to plan out an intended programme, then fill in the detail to be covered. This should be done in a progressive logical way so that the mind does not have to waste energy in drastic refocusing from one style of thought to another. For example, a secondary school child could arrange to revise chemistry followed by physics, then biology, geography, history, and so on.

Physical surroundings

There are two schools of thought about noise when studying. Some say there shouldn't be any, but others find relief in quiet constant background noise, such as the hum of distant traffic or quiet music. Many, such as my own teenage children, said that they liked to study to loud music, but, as a parent, I remained sceptical as to whether they were doing their best work at those times.

A heavy meal causes blood to flow away from the brain to assist the digestive organs, and makes you feel sleepy; the same results come from a hot bath (or drinking alcohol). Too comfortable a chair, too warm a room, poor light, or not enough fresh air, can all handicap study.

It helps continuity when the studying can always be done in the same place, so, if you can, spare a little space for your child. When a child can go to her familiar chair or desk, pick up the pencil from where she left it, and take up her ideas again from where she left them, her settling down time will be much reduced. If the study area can be organised in such a way that it only needs the arrival of the child to complete the familiar set up, then the processes of learning will flow almost automatically.

Remembering

There are often good reasons for forgetting things, or remembering them wrongly. A child soon forgets something that he doesn't like or finds boring. Looking back, you may recall that sometimes, when you'd finished the task for which you'd learned something – an exam, perhaps – you seemed to forget what you'd learned as you left the room. Unless you used that particular learning again, you

How to study

- Children should purposefully skim the work to be done so that they have a rough idea of what is to be covered. Directed effort, with an end-product, is better than vague searching. For example, a little child could make an effort to learn the letter B rather than attempting many different letters at the same time.
- Try to relate new material to what the child already knows. For example, John's splashing in the sink has taught him a lot about water movement. Show him how it balances itself in both arms of a U-shaped transparent plastic tube – the beginnings of physics.
- Learning is easier and better in comprehensible chunks, rather than unrelated fragments. Get Mary to read the whole piece regularly, not just a bit at a time. If possible, aim for peace and plenty of time so you aren't cut short. But longer works, such as books, may be read a chapter at a time.
- Half-understood words or passages should be looked up as you come across them. It's much easier to forget what you are supposed to be learning when you think you understand, but you're not quite sure. If they're taught to do it, children soon get in the habit of looking words up in their dictionaries.
- Get older children to summarise, in their own words, what they're reading or have listened to. This guarantees that they're having to think it through. Also, get them to emphasise the main points or principles, so that they become really involved with it. Most students know that it's a good idea to write down the essential facts about a subject on a postcard, which can then be carried around.
- Children can say what they've learned out loud,

even to themselves. This soon shows up the bits they're not quite clear about. Small children often do this quite naturally, unless they're made to feel embarrassed about talking to themselves. It is useful, though, at any age.

- Mnemonic systems can be helpful in a difficult situation, where there are unrelated lists to be remembered. We use one for the music scale, for example – Good Boys Deserve Fruit Always – though many music teachers believe that this type of rote learning may hinder a deeper musical appreciation.

possibly lost it altogether. On the other hand, an unfinished task has a sort of hangover effect – it stays on to be remembered, a phenomenon well documented in experimental psychology. So a good tip for both young and old is to leave your work not quite finished at the end of the day; the next day you'll then find it easier to pick up the threads again.

Reading

There are ways of reading that can speed up comprehension so that the reader gets the author's message quickly and accurately. *Use Your Head* by Tony Buzan describes many ways of improving reading and studying. With practice, it's possible to take in greater gulps of words at a time, instead of reading each word separately. Then, instead of reading across the lines of print, you can skim a page downwards, to see roughly what's on it. Don't feel inhibited about using your finger to guide your eyes. If you want to see some part of it in more detail, you can always go back for another look. Bright children are well able to start such speed-reading by the time they reach secondary school.

A PARENTS' GROUP

Good cooperation between a child's school and her home is usually the case, but there are exceptions, when parents and teachers just don't seem to be on the same wavelength. Sometimes, if parents have particular educational interests and the head teacher is either too overloaded with work or isn't interested in that area, then the parents have to act independently. For example, parents who believe their children are in need of extra educational help may choose to pool their resources to provide it for them. If this is the case for you, and you would like to get such a parents' group going, here are the sorts of things you might consider doing:

- Have parent education meetings, either listening to experts or trying out educational projects with your children.
- Compile a newsletter, in which the children take part, and which circulates ideas of interest.
- Establish where the local resources, such as special library facilities, are to be found.
- Organise field trips for parents and children, preferably with someone who can talk about the subject of the visit.
- Talk about the problems you have in common.
- The parents who start it should be those who have the time and energy to stay with the project and see it through.
- Form a committee made up of concerned parents, teachers or other people in the community. Select a temporary chairperson, to get the ball rolling, and sort out a plan of action. Then start with a meeting in someone's house to organise your group better. Have a theme that someone will speak on, with a discussion to follow. Keep a record of suggestions for activities and needs that are made at the meeting.
- Let tact be the order of the day. Keep the school informed and involved, as far as you can, while you're getting settled. Ask them for help, such as contacting

other parents who may be interested. The school is
more than likely to be on your side; after all, you're all
after the educational welfare of the children. Ask
parents who are interested to sign a list and to suggest
other potential members.

- Divide up the chores between subgroups; for example,
  you should have people specifically in charge of
  finance, community resources, liaison or special needs.
  Someone with legal knowledge can be very useful too.
  Decide how much you'll need to cover your expenses,
  so that you can charge a non-profitmaking
  membership fee. Perhaps the school would help out
  here. Decide on a contact address, and change it as
  little as possible so that newcomers can join in easily.

8
INTO BOOKS

Only a small part of the information necessary for learning to read comes from the printed page; most of it comes from listening and talking. Parents can help to bridge the gap between spoken and written language since the closer the child's spoken language is to what she sees on the printed page, the easier it will be for her to read. Bombarding a child with speech can be too much – it's quality, and her own participation in it, that counts.

You can encourage your child to be clear in what she says, for example, by trying to get her to put her message in a different way. The mental exercise will help her to extend her thinking. This talk between three-year-old Barbara and her mother may not seem much, but it shows that her ideas are getting a little clearer:

Barbara The milkman's come with the milk.

Mother Ah, but where did he get it from, I wonder.
Barbara Well, you know, cows. Well, they do it.
Mother What do cows do?
Barbara Well, you get milk from them.
Mother And then?
Barbara Well, it goes into bottles and we get it.
Mother Tell me about how it gets into the bottles.
Barbara (thinking quickly) The milkman squeezes it in.

The two most important aspects of talking with a child are the topic of the conversation and who's participating; the topic must be interesting to the child, and the adult should be someone who is important to him. Parents must really listen and respond carefully. For example, John, who was nearly three, was playing with his toy cars on the floor while his father watched from his armchair.

John That car's broken.
Father (coming over) Let's have a look. Oh! It's not broken, it's a truck and the platform tips up. See how it goes.
John Let me, let me.
Father (handing it back) Find something for the truck to carry, so you can see how it works.
John (showing his new learning) This truck's mine and I'm not going to.
Father What will you do then?
John (keeping his end up) I'm putting this truck on top of another truck!

John had got the idea of using the truck for carrying things; he'd shown his growing independence by refusing his father's advice, then gone one better by having the truck itself carried. His father couldn't help laughing with him at John's delight in his cleverness.

Psychologically speaking, printed words aren't quite the same as spoken ones. They are much more complicated to interpret. When you read, the translation from print to meaning happens in two ways; letters have first to be understood as sounds, and then as words. Your eyes dart about seeing how the letters lie on the page and sneaking a look at what is coming next, while your mind is working out what those collections of marks mean. A child has to learn that reading is knowing what to 'sound' and what to ignore. It isn't only a matter of decoding marks into spoken language, though; it's a skill of communication. Each person has his own way of using and controlling this skill.

When a beginning reader reads aloud to you, don't just listen to see whether she's doing it correctly or not, so that you can put her right. Listen to what she says; then, when she's wrong, let her join in so that she learns self-correction. Try not to be negative in your criticism, such as saying 'No, you shouldn't say the "d" in Wednesday'; instead say something like 'Try the word again, just as you usually say it.'

Sometimes children make a stab at a word they don't know, using the rules from the other words they do know, such as when a toddler says 'I didded it'. Though this approach may produce the wrong results in our illogical English language, it shows the beginnings of an awareness that print carries a message. It also shows that the child is using her intelligence to learn to read, and such an effort should be warmly encouraged. Parents have to reassure beginners that reading is for pleasure, and have to help them to want to learn to read for themselves. Reading aloud to little ones helps them to get that feeling, from the very earliest weeks – even if they don't understand a word. A small child gets to know the rhythm and structure of written language from this, so that when she gets to read for herself she'll be better at the anticipation part of the reading job. Book language is really something special.

A study in Scotland by Dr Margaret Clark on children who could read fluently before they started school brought out some features of early reading that parents should know about. These children, who had learned at home, were better at reading silently than children who had learned to read in front of the class at school. They took more pleasure in it and were also better at spelling, since, all the time they were learning to read, their parents had helped them to write too. They had been given blackboards and chalk to work with, and lots of paper and pencils. As a result they had become sensitive to the way words are made up of letters, and to how they should sound, and so they made a great effort to get it right.

When children are learning to read, and as they move on to tackle harder books, they will progress better if they have instant assistance from an interested adult to help them when they get stuck. This is where parents have the edge over teachers; while a teacher simply can't provide that kind of service to every one of her class when they need it, parents – or any other adult who's minding the child – can do it. With a free library service, it's not a matter of money or social class; it's a matter of what parents do together with their children. Where written and spoken language are experienced by a child as everyday happenings, in a warm and accepting family, her education will have been given a great start. Children who learn to read early and with pleasure usually have parents who feel the same way about the joy of reading.

THE METHODS SCHOOLS USE

There have been at least 13 innovations in teaching children to read within the last quarter century. The most noticeable was the initial teaching alphabet (ita). For this, a new alphabet was devised so that children could spell the words the way they sounded, like tuf instead of tough. This was found to be a help to slow learners, but did not benefit bright children, and schools have now dropped it. There have also been a variety of colour-coded teaching designs, and even programmed learning with machines, but these proved too expensive for most schools. The following are the three current basic teaching methods.

Look and say (whole word or sentence)
The idea behind this method is to establish a relationship between what the child sees (and remembers) and what he hears, so that he forms a chain of mental connections, in the way adults do when they read. The child is presented

with a word or phrase by the teacher and repeats it aloud; the words the teacher chooses are those she thinks will interest the child. Teachers usually ask children to write the words at the same time, to build up a feeling for them by the movements made in writing. A child can get on very quickly and get more pleasure from reading this way, but the method often produces poor spellers, and even good silent readers may later be seen making movements with their mouths and throats.

Phonic method
Here the child is taught to recognise sounds from letters, and to make them up into words, like c-a-t spells cat. It begins by emphasising the words that follow well defined rules, then goes on to introduce less regular words like 'would'. The material to be learned, though, has to be carefully organised. For example, it can be grouped into what teachers call 'magic e' or same-sound letter patterns, such as meat and peep; into soft or hard letter sounds, such as sage and gate; or into words that are formed when you add an 'e' to others, such as care and fire.

The problem with this method is that it is less immediately rewarding to children, so that they are less keen to learn than with the look and say method. But it does produce good spellers, and possibly helps towards a better understanding of language.

Eclectic methods
Many schools take what they want from the above two methods and mix them as they see fit. In fact, most parents and teachers do this to some extent. It's important to realise that no one method of reading can suit all children. Reading is entirely a matter for the individual, as it isn't just a matter of decoding marks on the page, but is a constructive thinking process. Reading 'between the lines' is part of normal meaningful reading.

More advanced reading
The fluent reader has abandoned the word-by-word or

symbol-by-symbol approach; she skims the lines, reading for meaning and looking for familiar sentence structures. Gradually, her response to what she sees becomes automatic and she only hesitates to decipher slowly when she comes to an unfamiliar word or sentence structure.

DYSLEXIA

Even the most intelligent children can have difficulty in learning to read and write. The word that is often used to cover the whole range of such problems is dyslexia, or word blindness. Interpretations of this condition range from the mildest difficulty with reading to very specific problems such as a child's inability to translate the visual symbols on the paper – the letters of the alphabet – into words. But of all children with reading problems, those with dyslexia are only a small minority. To be dyslexic a child must not only have difficulty in reading, but must also have an average or superior intelligence and normal functioning senses. Other members of a dyslexic child's family are often found to have the same problem, and the disorder is most frequently found in boys. The actress Susan Hampshire, who is dyslexic herself, has suggested in her book *Susan's Story* that 12.5 per cent of all children are dyslexic to some extent.

However, the diagnosis of dyslexia is sometimes used as a catch-all term for children's reading problems, many of which may come from other sources. A child of three and a half came to me recently for psychological asssessment because he was said to 'have dyslexia'. Indeed, the little boy was a very slow learner, but then one might say that all three and a half year olds are not very good at reading and so 'have dyslexia'.

However, there are some fairly clear signs of dyslexia, which parents can look for if they are worried about their child's reading level, and the earlier they are spotted the better are his chances of improvement. Though children who learn to read normally can also come up with similar problems, they will get over them and make good progress, but the dyslexic seems to get stuck and can't get on without help.

Many sufferers seem to have difficulty in interpreting the letters of a word in the right order. The world 'saw', for example, may be read as 'was', and the word 'no' as 'on', or 'dog' as 'god'. You may find that your child is writing as though looking in a mirror, so that 'dog' then becomes 'gob'. Such children need a lot of patient teaching. By sheer hard work a dyslexic child may learn that p-i-g spells pig, only to forget it all the next (if not the same) day. Sometimes a dyslexic child's spelling can be so bizarre that even the most empathetic reader can't make it out. These spelling mistakes often carry on into adult life, even when the person has learned to read with useful skill. Dyslexic children usually have difficulty in working out laterality – left/right and up/down – and they can't re-find their place on the page if their attention is lost for a moment. They may have very poor short-term memories, forgetting what you've just told them, often can't seem to be able to keep still, and tire very easily. As toddlers, they may have been late in learning to fasten buttons and put their clothes on properly.

Reading difficulties may not necessarily be due to dyslexia, though, but can be because of any of the following reasons:

- Problems with speaking, hearing or seeing.
- Emotional disturbance, such as insecurity.
- Prolonged illness.
- Discouragement.
- Poor teaching.

Unfortunately, whatever the reason, poor reading skills can spill over to affect a child's learning in other areas, such as arithmetic, or all round, so that she feels low about her general ability to learn. She may also take to misbehaving, possibly opting out of classroom projects, which isolates her even further. Bright children are particularly good at hiding their basic reading problem. They can find a thousand excuses, such as going to the toilet just when you want them to read, or losing their glasses, and so on; such a system works in a busy classroom, but of course it only makes their situation worse by delaying the help they so badly need.

It is often impossible to find the root cause of dyslexia. There is a theory that certain parts of the brain that deal with symbols and left–right choices simply fail to mature normally. Whatever the cause, the best anyone can do is to try to relieve the immediate problems, although it is also important to help a dyslexic child realise that his difficulty is not a stigma. There are no easy cures available, and though educational gadgets may offer variety, there is no substitute for a specially trained teacher with infinite patience. But, because of the shortage of such teachers, parents may find that they have to shoulder most, if not all, of the burden themselves.

Here are some ideas about what to do if you think your child may be dyslexic:

- Consult the school, which is likely to be sympathetic and offer help.
- If the school indicates that, in their eyes, your child is simply 'thick' or 'spoilt', ask for him to be tested by an educational psychologist. Your local education authorities should be able to help you. If there is difficulty, you could have your child assessed privately.
- Contact your nearest dyslexia organisations. They can provide assessment, advice, teaching help and an understanding ear. They will also tell you the truth.

Even when a child who has difficulty with reading is referred to as dyslexic by a psychologist or teacher, it does not mean that he can't improve over time – or that the diagnosis is correct. Any child with normal hearing and sight can learn to read reasonably well, even though his development may be slow or uneven, and bright dyslexic children usually have good comprehension to help them. This problem does not necessarily inhibit creative writing – W.B. Yeats, the poet, and Hans Christian Andersen, the Danish storyteller, were both dyslexic. Some children, with

great grit and determination, go on to study extensively for
professions such as medicine or dentistry. But others will
always have difficulty in writing a note or reading a
timetable.

There are some home exercises you can try, but if in
doubt do seek the help of an expert; not all parents have
the patience of saints. Though learning to read is best
encouraged by the pleasure it brings, it is likely to be hard
work for the dyslexic. The adult in charge has to provide
lots of breaks, a variety of approaches and lavish
encouragement. Try reading one page of a book (of a
suitable level) together, then talk about what you have
read. Ask the child to imagine what comes next before he
goes on, so that he has to think forwards. Other points to
remember are to listen to the child reading without
correcting him for as long as you can, and not to offer false
praise. Make spellings so easy that he's bound to succeed.
Concerted effort is important. It is important to get
specialist opinion and help if you can (see the useful
addresses at the back of the book).

SHOULD PARENTS TEACH READING?

Many parents are anxious that if they teach their children
to read before starting school it will cause problems later
on. Some feel it will interfere with the child's normal
development, and others that the school will look less
favourably on their child. In fact, parents often don't tell
the school that the child can read as they feel embarrassed
about it. The crime writer Agatha Christie's parents
refused to let her read before the age of seven as they
thought it wasn't good for young children; but she, being a
bright child, wrote in her autobiography that she taught
herself before the age of five.

The idea of 'reading readiness' – that if you teach a child
to read before she's 'ready' she will suffer from emotional
problems – has been around for some time. This idea took
hold in America for many years, so that some school areas
still try to prevent children from learning to read until they

are seven years old. At the opposite extreme, Glen Doman's *Teach Your Baby to Read* had some babies recognising words on cards before a year old, though the long-term value of this exercise is less than clear. From a commonsense point of view, it is clearly nonsense to say that children aren't ready to read when they can already read fluently.

Teachers vary in their reaction to the news that a five year old can read. Some are excited, and see it as giving the child great scope, but others are either indifferent or else feel it will leave the child bored. Some primary teachers unfortunately aren't very interested in a child's learning experiences outside school, feeling that their education begins when they enter the school's portals.

Parents usually know which school their child will go to when she's five, and can sound out the school's attitude. Not that they should prevent a child from reading, even if the school disapproves, but they can help to smooth over her entry to school. Parents who don't give the teacher the information she should have, for whatever reason, are not helping her to do her job properly. It also means that the teacher learns not to trust the parents. Obviously the changeover has to be handled with tact, but if your child can read before starting school, then say so.

If a child isn't interested in reading, then there's no point in forcing her to try before she starts school. It's important that the child's early experiences of reading be successful; a child learns to read by reading and wanting to read more. Parents' anxieties about reading can cause children to feel failures, which may prove to be an emotional drag on their learning. It's extremely unlikely that a child with normal sight will have physical problems in learning to decode printing, although it is possible; it is more likely that there are other reasons for difficulty with reading.

Try to stop them

Very few parents actually set out to teach reading to uninterested infants. Quite the reverse – clever children who learn to read when they are still toddlers often seem to

What you can do to help reading

- Talk and listen to your baby from the time of birth.
- Tell him stories.
- Show him pictures and talk about them together.
- Encourage him to talk about what he's been doing.
- Point out words wherever you are – on television or in the street.
- Try to use proper sentences when talking to him.
- Teach nursery rhymes, or any other rhymes with a clear rhythm; sing and do the actions.
- Teach colour names.
- Encourage him to speak clearly.
- Board games like snakes and ladders help coordinate eye and hand movements.
- Tap out simple rhythms together.
- Put up the names of things, printed in large letters on cards, over everyday objects – SINK on the sink, or BED over his bed.
- Above all, listen to your child's attempts at reading. The more he reads the better. Once he's finished a book give him another, especially one with pictures that are big, clear and relevant to him.
- Take it easy. Over-anxious parents can put a child off reading. If you are in any doubt as to a child's readiness to read, wait till you can discuss it with his teacher. Sing and tell him stories instead.

do so by demanding that their parents teach them. Right from the beginning these early-readers use their new skill to extend their knowledge, sometimes by means of newspapers and sometimes by books. If you read a quality paper at home, it's a good idea to buy a simpler one for a while, for your early-reader to practise on. Make sure you take your child to the local library and show her how to choose books. Most libraries have a special advice librarian for children, who can be very helpful.

Our great-grandparents knew the pleasure of reading aloud to each other. There is every reason to go on doing this with children, even when they can read for themselves. The extra benefit is that now the child can read to you, then talk about what either of you have read. But by five years old an advanced child is beginning to get pleasure from reading alone. Give him time and peace to get to know books by himself, as well as enjoying them together.

Bright children catch on to the idea of reading from many places. They see words on television, for instance – advertisements often show a word, then say it for the viewer. Later on a child may see the advertised product on the supermarket shelves or in the kitchen, and can again practise looking at the name and saying it. Some children learn from the titles of audio-tapes or discs, by memorising the whole title and reading the simpler words. Words and sounds are everywhere; bright children very soon begin to put them together.

What should they read?
Local libraries and schools very often group children's books in a way that adults think are suitable for children of certain ages. Some schools and libraries will only allow children to pick books out of the age-group that has been earmarked for them. But children who can read fluently are often interested in much more than children's books can offer them, and may be irritated by the simplified vocabulary of children's books for their own age group. Sometimes it may be difficult to persuade a school to allow an infant access to the junior bookshelves, but with a parent's membership card there's no problem at the local library.

Let children choose to read what they want. If they don't understand the book they've taken out, they'll either skip the hard parts or take it back. If a five year old picks up Tolstoy, does it really matter if he has to take it back the next day as a mistake? After all, we learn from our mistakes.

WRITING

Reading and writing skills don't necessarily develop together; this is because they make use of different psychological procedures. Being able to read means sorting out letters and their meanings and remembering them; being able to write means fine control of finger and arm movements, and the skill to reproduce letters. Some very young, and undeniably gifted, children may even be able to read by three years old, but they won't be able to write then. A five year old may read fluently, but still find difficulty in tying a bow in her hair.

The beginnings of writing come from painting and drawing. Sit down with your child as soon as she can barely grasp a crayon, and show her how pleasant it is to draw. Then you can print in big letters underneath her drawing what she says it is. In time she'll start to go over your printing with her crayon.

When a child has a vocabulary of about 100 words she should be given a special notebook with a letter written on each page in alphabetical order. Then, when she's stuck on how to write a word, she can usually show you the first letter and you can help her with the rest.

Some schools try to coordinate the learning of reading and writing. This can make life difficult for a child who's been reading well since she was four but who can't write well; she may even be expected to pull her writing level up to her reading level. What may happen is that she struggles with the writing, but can't get it right because her reading is so advanced. As a result she becomes unhappy at school, her all-round progress suffers – and nobody knows why.

Children should be encouraged, not pressured, to write as clearly and carefully as they can, so that they can see the words they know in their own writing. When they make mistakes they know about them, and can work with their parents to correct them. Let the child rub out the wrongly spelled word and put in the right spelling. It will give her a lot of satisfaction. Teachers sometimes insist on crossings-out being kept in for inspection, and they also teach the children to cross out in an approved manner. But for keen children it's just a mark of shame to keep their mistakes on view, and this method doesn't encourage pride in a neat page.

There's been a great feeling for 'creative' writing in schools over the last few years, possibly at the expense of spelling and grammar. However, there may be a way out of the dilemma of whether you should inhibit your child's thoughts by insisting on correct English or let her slap down anything to promote her creativity. Children can speak out loud to a listener or use a tape-recorder for their wildest fantasies, then, like any other craftsman, they can use their skills at writing to get it down on paper. It would also help children to become aware of the differences between spoken and written language.

Some children have particularly strong visual awareness, which helps them in reading and writing, while others have to set out consciously to learn the rules like spelling and how parts of words fit together. The wider the child's experience of hearing speech and playing with writing materials, the more capable he will be of tackling the complexities of English spelling.

Handwriting skills

Schools have been taking an easier attitude towards handwriting skills, as many of the traditional uses for such skills, such as for letter writing and clerking, have been taken over by typewriters, computers or word processors. Beautiful writing is thus no longer the widely valued skill it once was. Bright children soon pick up this feeling that handwriting is not very important and, particularly as it can be a slow and tedious process, show little enthusiasm for learning it.

Handwriting involves not only the fingers that hold the pencil, but the whole body. A child needs a comfortable relaxed but supported position for writing. To begin with he

needs a table and chair of a suitable height; later on he will
be able to write on different surfaces at different heights
and under different conditions. During writing the hand
and arm should be capable of free movement and the
pencil held in the correct way. Right- and left-handed
children have different needs. The right-handed child
should place his paper parallel to the edge of the table or at
a slight angle. The left-handed child places his paper on
the left and at an angle of about 45 degrees. He also needs
to hold his pencil further away from the point than the
right-handed child, so that he does not cover what he's
writing with his hand.

There are two important skills a child needs for writing.

- Copying skill. It's difficult for a very young child to
  focus on individual letters and write them down in the
  right order to form a word or sentence; instead you can
  ask the child to write over or trace words you have
  written for him. The child can then progress on to
  copying underneath your writing, and later on he can
  copy on another page. The further away his writing is
  from yours, the harder he has to work at remembering
  what he's seen and the order of the letters. Bigger
  chunks of writing to copy mean that he also has to
  develop the skill of finding the right place on the page
  in order to go on to copy the next letter or word.
- Pencil control and letter formation. When a child learns
  to form letters correctly, he is also learning to recognise
  them more easily in his reading – bad writing habits
  lead to confusion in reading. For example, the letters 'b'
  and 'd' are very often confused by children who are not
  dyslexic. This can happen particularly if they're taught
  to draw a circle first and then add a stick to the
  left-hand side for 'b' and right-hand side for 'd'. But if
  they start with the stick for 'b' and the circle for 'd' they
  learn to form quite different letters more easily.

Teachers often feel strongly about punctuation, although
children usually show when they're ready to learn it. You
can see when their writing becomes more fluent, with the

word 'and' used over and over again to join up sentences; that's the time to bring in full stops and capital letters. Bright children soon get the idea of pauses and commas. If the child is unconvinced that punctuation works, read his piece back to him without it. But patience and praise are the mainstays of improving punctuation. Don't spoil a child's work with your own comments or marks – sometimes turning a blind eye to mistakes can be more encouraging. Very early mistakes, such as no spacing between words or mirror-writing, normally correct themselves. Help the child to find his own errors.

The trend in teaching children to write has recently been to encourage them to write using their imagination, interests and experiences – to be creative. This is a vital and welcome change from the drudgery of hours of copying that children used to undergo. But don't expect too much; not every child is a creative genius or has a free-flowing mind. Most children's work, even that of bright children, is pretty conventional. However some creative children do have very fertile imaginations and are so keen to get a story down that their handwriting skills (or lack of them) are an encumbrance; they may feel that by the time they have painstakingly formed the letters in a legible way, they have lost the excitement, and perhaps it's not worth the trouble. A typewriter or, better still, a word processor, may then help a lot.

Even little children can learn to type quite quickly and, once they have mastered it, it can be a handy skill for life. It can certainly be a very much quicker way for a speedy five-year-old thinker to commit his thoughts to paper than handwriting. Critics feel that this will ruin the formation of a beautiful script, but on the other hand, creative thinking abilities are surely at least as important in the long run. Children's typewriters can be bought quite cheaply. In later years a child's teacher can be very appreciative of typed essays to mark rather than scruffy handwritten ones.

What you can do to help writing

- Let the baby 'draw' on thick paper with a pencil or crayon, or on a blackboard with chalks.
- Help guide his hand around shapes as he gets older.
- Get him to practise drawing a straight line.
- Start him on simple jigsaws.
- Leave him alone to draw if he's absorbed.
- Ask him what he's just looked at in a simple picture.
- Find toys or objects that he can sort into sets – say by colour – as he explains what he's doing. 'This is a round shape, it's a circle, it's red', etc.
- Play 'join the dots' games.
- Get him to run toy cars along painted tracks.
- Playing paper and pencil games such as noughts and crosses (tic, tac, toe) can help.
- Tracing patterns gives practice in moving both eye and hand from left to right, up and down, in upward and downward curves, and through right angles. After a while the tracing paper can be removed and the child asked to copy simple shapes, such as:

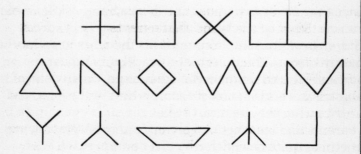

This can be done first with matches, then by drawing them.

- Draw simple shapes with a bit missing and ask your child to fill them in, like these:

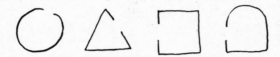

- Ask the child to copy repetitive patterns like these:

- Always have thick soft pencils or crayons and plenty of paper handy.
- Personalise the child's efforts by giving him very thin (maybe home-made) exercise books, so that the child can fill them up quickly and get more satisfaction.

ARITHMETIC

During the 1980s new ideas took the teaching of numbers by storm. Most of the 'sums' that parents used to do as children have gone into disuse, while the new maths has taken the focus off numbers and put it on to logical relationships and mathematical language. So, instead of doing sums, children now measure rooms and desks, and compare what they've discovered.

Parents and teachers, caught up in this whirlwind, are sometimes quite bewildered by the new approach – why not teach tables anyway? All sorts of educational teaching toys and equipment have come on to the market, and it's often difficult to tell if they're worth the expense.

Where do you start?

Babies start to learn numbers by listening to parents counting things, such as fingers or steps, over and over again. Many nursery rhymes have counting in them, and bright children love these. Soon they can write some numbers as they say them, which is something to be encouraged. The language of mathematics can thus emerge quite naturally in a lively home. Professor Seymour Papert, the mathematician, says that a home should be mathematically literate; this means that, just as children are expected and do learn their letters, they should do the same with numbers.

There's no need to force early arithmetical understanding, though; it's all there in everyday conversations. Every time you say 'more than' or 'less than', you are teaching. Parents can bargain with children by saying things such as 'If you eat up two more spoonfuls of dinner, you can have one sweet.' A word of warning here, though; since children can tackle mathematical ideas without understanding the concepts behind them, parents sometimes think their children are cleverer than they really are, and may expect too much from them. Remember, even a simple sum requires quite a lot of consideration. Firstly, a child has to understand the meaning of adding up. Secondly, he has to be able to carry it out mentally. Thirdly, he has to cope with symbolic notation of $+$ and $=$, and fourthly, he has to understand the often confusing wording of 2 and 2 are 4. So you have to try to help him in each of these four steps.

What really matters, right from the beginning, is the child's mental approach to arithmetic. It should be seen as a pleasant thing to do – really fun, and not too difficult. So many parents give children the message that it's so hard – especially for girls – that they learn to be frightened of numbers. Bright children have a real capacity to enjoy exercising their mental ability; they like doing sums and feeling good about it, even before they fully understand what they're doing. What puts many children off, though, is the old-fashioned grind of arithmetic exercises. So, keep your touch light.

Space and weight

The idea of shapes comes most easily from puzzles, or sorting things, such as the matching involved in some toys and games. Matching a shape to its hole teaches children about up and down, across, sizes and relationships between parts. The 'rightness' of the successful move is very satisfying and makes a nice balance to more open-ended kinds of play.

The familiar shape-sorting toy for a baby is one where he has to put a block of wood into the correctly shaped slot, and there are many variants on the theme. Circles are easier to insert than squares, and then triangles. So if the toy has all three, it might take time and much frustration for a very young child to master the whole pattern. Separate shapes on each block are easier and better to start with.

Toddlers can manage puzzles of two kinds, though some are more interested in this activity than others. One kind is an island puzzle, where each piece is complete; it may be an animal, for example, which fits into its own shaped hole in the board. The other kind is the jigsaw, where the pieces must slot together correctly to make a whole picture; bright little ones can start using a jigsaw of about three pieces from about 18 months old.

Bring in as much variety as you can think of – different coloured cut-out numbers, paper with different sized squares, and different kinds of things to count and move around. Think up practical exercises to do, like seeing how much water from one jar fills up another, or how many beans you can put in different pots.

Little children need lots of practice at comparing sizes and shapes. The best way of starting is to get children to measure with parts of their bodies, such as the number of hand-spans, thumb-widths or foot-lengths that make up a table or anything else. This provides both mental and physical gymnastics. As soon as they want to they can

---

Some tips with puzzles for little ones

- Make sure the pieces are big enough to be handled by the child; they should not be so small that they could be swallowed.
- Colours should be bright and clear.
- The pieces should fit into the wells easily.
- Tell stories along with pictures of familiar scenes.
- Don't finish it for the child, but make suggestions and let the child believe he has done it.
- Praise the attempt.

---

move on to using rulers, measuring tapes, etc. Then they can make a diagram of what they've found, and draw simple block graphs that can be coloured. It gives a child great satisfaction to see his work pinned up on the wall.

Weighing things is a bit more complicated. Children have to get the idea of weight and balance first. For this they need practice at feeling the heaviness of things, and then weighing them to compare them more accurately. Start by using some simple balance scales to get first the idea of heavier and lighter, and then the idea of equilibrium. When a child seems to understand these concepts you can move on to a spring balance to see how weights are measured on a linear scale. Even quite clever children, though, are usually well into school before they understand about standardised weights.

The discovery method

One problem with some of the new approaches to numbers was that teachers sometimes took the ideas too literally, which brought about some failures in using them. The idea of discovery was that children should learn for themselves by handling materials and tackling practical problems; in this way they should be using their own brains, rather than being told by adults exactly what to do. But what sometimes happened was that children were given a lot of

teaching equipment and simply told, without any
guidance, 'Go on, discover!'

But it doesn't work like that. A child can't grasp the
basics – ideas that great thinkers took centuries to work out
– all alone. Children need guidance and help in
understanding these ideas. This neither means spelling out
exactly what to do every time, nor does it mean closing the
door on the child's attempts at exploration. Teaching
mathematics is a two-way process between teacher and
child, and there has to be flexibility on both sides.

A fine example of such flexibility was shown by a teacher
who had an argument with a child who insisted that a
triangle only had two sides. First of all she tried to correct
the child by telling him that a triangle has three sides.
'But', he replied, 'it has two sides and a bottom.' She had to
agree that it was a way of seeing it. After all, we can't
assume that children can perceive geometrical objects as
floating in Euclidian space; they see triangles as standing
up, and so perhaps 'edge' is a better word to use than 'side'.

Child mathematicians

Bertrand Russell, the philosopher and mathematician,
once wrote: 'At the age of eleven I began Euclid with my
brother as tutor. This was one of the great events of my life,
as dazzling as first love. I had not imagined there was
anything so delicious in the world.'

There are a few brilliant children like Russell who are
quite fluent at number work by the time they reach school.
But, like the early reader, these children may have
problems, firstly in being believed and secondly in fitting
in with the level of the rest of the class. For example, an
eight-year-old mathematician might have to sit through a
long laboured explanation about prime factors, even though
he'd discovered them for himself a year or two ago. What is
he to do during the lesson?

Mathematical children can be of any personality or
either sex, but they all love numbers. Some have very
strong feelings about their 'own' special numbers such as 7
or 3. They can add, subtract, multiply and divide in their

What to do to help with arithmetic

- Encourage the baby to play with water. Start with the bathwater, to get the idea of floating, sinking, filling up cups and so on. Later on you can use ice cubes, or colour the water, to encourage ideas of amounts and space.
- Let the child play with flour and water dough, squidging it through his fingers making shapes, and dividing it up, getting a feeling of quantity.
- Have a sandpit if you can, with cups in it. Even a small amount of sand on a big tray is sufficient, placed where it doesn't matter if it spills.
- Toy bricks provide one of the longest lasting and most valuable toys for learning arithmetic. You will need at least 60. They should be in proportion to each other, so they fit together smoothly and look and feel nice. Different colours on the sides of the bricks add a lot to the fun of learning.
- Fitting-together toys, like post-boxes or nesting-dolls, give practice in hand and eye coordination. This goes for jigsaw puzzles and other toys that are designed to match up.
- Some toys hook together to make longer or shorter lines (e.g. toy trains), some can be threaded together (e.g. cotton reels) and some can be stacked on to an upright stick (e.g. plastic hoops).
- Sorting-out games, like miniature cars or farm animals, give children practice in classifying.
- Give children different shapes to feel; talk about how shape affects balance and working, and how they feel about what it looks like.
- Play shops, buying and selling things like food or lengths of material; use pretend money, or tokens like tiddlywink discs for it.
- Play dice-throwing games like snakes and ladders or ludo, especially ones that involve counting.
- See that the child's measuring devices, such as balances and weights, are accurate.

heads from an early age. Later on, should the teacher oblige them to do it in his way, stage by stage, they can get confused at having to remember what seems pointless to them, and may even seem stupid. It's like being obliged to do gymnastics with crutches when you are able to jump and run with ease and grace.

Watch out for thinking questions from your child, such as 'What happens if we put 3 instead of 6?' or 'What happens if we turn the figure upside down?' or 'Let's use letters instead of numbers.' Mathematical children don't usually wait to be taught how to work things out; they search out problems and answers for themselves. What is a problem to the ordinary child may be obviously simple to the mathematical one. The most valuable intellectual need for such a child is a good stock of problems that will challenge him; there are quite a number of 'problem' books in libraries and bookshops. As he gets older, the child can make use of old examination papers and even university texts, and perhaps his teacher can arrange for him to sit in with an older group for maths.

There are competitions for the able young mathematician, such as the International Olympiad, which is now over a quarter of a century old. Although Russia has some special schools for the mathematically gifted, there are few in the rest of the world. Other nations don't seem to go in for that kind of hot-house treatment of children, and there is little evidence to show that they're really beneficial to their pupils in the long term.

9
WILLINGLY TO SCHOOL

Education is about helping each individual fulfil their potential, and that includes those whose potential is high. This chapter brings together some of the important new findings about the educational needs of our brightest children, and about the kind of education that is appropriate for their capacity to learn.

Few teachers will find themselves with a Mozart or an Einstein in their class, but they will all be in charge of bright children at some time – and these may be yours. Children do their best at school when parents and teachers work in harmony, and when each understands what the others are trying to do. This begins when a child starts nursery school, and it goes right on till the end of secondary school in much the same way.

It sometimes happens that parents and teacher may not agree on what a child is capable of – one person's geese are another's swans – and children may not behave the same way at school as at home. For example, a bright little lad who is thriving and into everything at home may try to please the teacher with what he thinks is wanted of him at school. So he may cut down on asking the questions that come to his mind, or do his homework exactly as he thinks is required – and no more – even though he's really capable of much more imaginative and interesting work. In this way, parents and teacher are both justified in seeing quite different pictures of him. A six year old was heard by his mother reading aloud in a flat uninteresting style, though he had often read to her with life and enthusiasm. 'Why are you doing that?' she asked. 'When I do that at school', he replied, 'teacher says "Very good".'

Appearance counts too. When the teacher sees her pupil clean, tidy and ready to work, she's more likely to see him as bright than the one who's a mess and doesn't seem to care about school. She's also more likely to treat him more favourably, without even being aware of it herself. Although parents may not care much about their child's appearance themselves, it's a good idea to send your child to school looking ready for work. My bright daughter often questioned this idea, though, at her rather old-fashioned girls' academic school where uniform was strict. She would ask, for example, 'How does wearing a ring at school affect my ability to learn?' It doesn't, of course, but it does affect the teachers' view of children.

A teacher's ideas of who is bright and who isn't are very often influenced by the type of children who go to the school. In some areas, where parents are able to do a lot to help their children, the teacher may describe children as bright only when they do very well in tests and exams. As a result, some potentially high achieving children, who are not the best in that particular school, may be under-rated.

The opposite can happen in a school which draws children from culturally poor homes; teachers may feel that no bright child could come from such surroundings. Once, when I was looking for bright children for a research project, a headteacher said to me 'You'll not find any bright children in my school – they're all from council housing.' Parents have to work extra hard for their bright children if they go to a school where the headteacher has that kind of dismissive attitude.

The teacher's reactions to a child's culture can sometimes hamper his school progress. If, for example, an inner-city boy was to use, in a school essay, the language that came naturally to him at home, the teacher might find it grammatically incorrect and mark him down. When any child, however clever, constantly sees his spontaneous thoughts and ideas crossed out in red he may lose heart. Children with culturally different backgrounds need special care and encouragement from both parents and teachers; what it often means is that the disadvantaged child has to learn not one, but two codes of behaviour and language. The boyhood of Emlyn Williams, portrayed so beautifully in his book *The Corn is Green*, told how, as a Welsh-speaking boy struggling in an English language school, he was helped to success by a kind and interested teacher.

It can happen that a really bright child may find herself working below her ability in a lower stream of a rigidly organised school. This used to happen quite frequently when bright children were misplaced by the 11-plus exam, which made mistakes in about 10 per cent of all its selections. Thousands of children who should have gone to selective grammar schools were instead sent to unacademic secondary modern schools; there they began to think of themselves as failures and stopped using their intellectual abilities to the full, although they were perfectly capable of going to university.

Some writers such as Ivan Illich, who wrote *Deschooling Society*, believe that schools are organisations devoted to making future citizens conform to society's rules. Others say that schools have almost no effect, and that everything that helps a child to get on in the world comes from the home. But research by Professor Michael Rutter in London has found that all schools have measurable outlooks and practices, which have a considerable effect on their pupils, both in teaching and atmosphere – after all, pupils do spend a lot of their time there.

The way children feel about themselves and their abilities can have a marked influence on how they get on at school. They're not only sensitive to the way the teacher sees them, but also to their schoolmates' opinions. Gifted children, for example, may feel that they are looked on as odd, even in very academic schools. As a result, they may hide their exceptionality, believing that if they seem average they will make more friends. Parents should watch out for this, and give the child lots of support and love so that he can feel confident enough to shine in his own way – and still make friends.

It's strange how this situation only applies to children who are intellectually clever – brilliant athletes only ever seem to receive praise. Fortunately, as children get older, they usually become more accurate in judging how well they can do at school. For those who are lucky enough to have parents who really care, it's possible to get on with the job of being successful at school, and to feel good about it and about themselves.

MOTIVATION TO LEARN

The cornerstone of good learning is the will to learn – motivation. Many bright children are not motivated to learn, either at home or at school, and when they have fallen into a pattern of not achieving as much as they could it's not likely to right itself naturally. Parents and teachers then have to step in.

If a child is to do well, he must want to do well – you can take a horse to water but you can't make it drink. In educational terms you can provide your child with all the intellectual nourishment anyone could want – good quality toys, the finest schools and a lovely home – but you can't make him want to be successful. How does it happen, then, that some children are motivated to do well and some aren't?

Motivation is the result of a child coming to expect things because of what he does. A two year old, for example, can reasonably expect to build a pile of six bricks. He's not sure at first, of course, but when he does succeed he's most gratified, and may be spurred on to try seven bricks next time. But if he fails, his estimate of what he can do may take a tiny knock. Depending on the way he feels about it, he may try again and fail – causing another tiny knock – or succeed, and feel better about himself. He may fail because the bricks are not as well made as the last set he played with, but then his expectations would not be founded on a real situation. Or he may fail because he's over-reached himself. Either way, his expectations and hopes for his next tower-block may become a little lower as a result of his experience on this one.

In this trial and error way a child comes to judge what he can do, and when he might be able to do it. He'll use parents' and teachers' judgment a lot in helping to form his guidelines. For a child to do his best, you should encourage him to aim a bit higher next time, but his expectations should not be too high or too low – the judgment is a delicate one.

When parents and teachers expect too much of their child, so that he's bound to fail often, he can lose confidence in his own judgment and become more and more dependent on their ideas of what he can do. He may also see himself as a growing failure. Children who are recognised as gifted are in particular danger of this happening to them. They may, for example, be expected to be successful in everything they do. But children, like adults, have their ups and downs, and are better at some things than others.

Children can be taught to feel sure of what they can do, and so be helped towards wanting to do their best. Both motivation to do well and independence of thought stem from feelings of security and support, which are learned very early in life. This means giving the child a feeling of pride in the things that he does well, so that he can be sure that his parents' praise and attention will follow whenever he tries to do well. Parents play a very important part in a child's will to learn and succeed.

Those who, right from the start, see their children as independent little people allow them freer expression, are less critical and are more likely to have children who achieve well. Children of parents who use a lot of control, are over-protective and unwilling to reason with them generally do less well.

Many people who have eventually become eminent, and who must have been very bright children, didn't always do well at school – Einstein was one, Churchill another. But once they were motivated, there was no stopping them. A study of 400 prominent people found that, although they loved learning, three out of five were poor performers at school. If children seem to be failing at specific tasks, try a new approach. Get them to ask 'How can I do this?' instead of 'Can I do this?'

When children don't want to learn, there are usually good reasons for it. Sometimes it's because of emotional problems, but there are often more straightforward difficulties, such as those outlined below, stemming from the approach of parents and teachers to the business of learning.

Meaning

Where a child has more than one teacher – which is usually the case – some teaching may not seem to have any connection with the rest. What may happen is that the thinking skills that a child learns with one teacher don't seem to apply to another teacher's lessons. To the child, it may also seem that school learning doesn't connect up with 'real' life anyway, so that the whole thing becomes a pointless exercise. As tedious exercises are fortunately being used very much less in lessons, and teachers are getting together more in their approaches to children, this handicapping of a child's feeling for learning should also get less.

Learning has to be meaningful to the child, so you may have to point the meanings out. Take children to places where they can see what's taught at school being put into use. The most obvious connection is probably sums and money; don't do all the paying for the shopping yourself – let the child do it and make sure it's correct. Let him help with weighing for cooking and measuring for the new floor-covering, for example.

Tests

Some schools set weekly tests and marks, and bright children can find these irritating; they know how inadequate the tests are, and often what a waste of time they are too.

To some extent teachers have to give tests to find out how different members of the class are getting on, but they could be changed in style to increase the children's motivation. Rather than just asking for facts to be reproduced, tests can actually be creative, using the child's thinking skills and imagination. They can measure decision-making and judgment, which is much more interesting.

Most children can get bored with ordinary tests and, if so, they may show up poorly in them. If you think this may be a problem, talk about it with the teacher – tactfully.

Difficulty

More than most, really bright children get into the position where the learning is either too easy or too difficult for them. They have to proceed at their own rate, either skipping some stages that other children need to complete, or finding a challenge that they cannot meet. A teacher can easily over-estimate the ability of a very clever child, who may find the work too difficult at that time and give up trying. This can be a problem for children who are moved up a year or two and miss out on preparatory lessons. Parents may have to point this out to teachers – in the nicest possible way. Don't be too ambitious for your child, even though she may be very bright; she may be happier and learn better in a steady, less challenging class.

For example, Janice was a gifted little girl of six years old whose mother brought her to see me because of her temper tantrums. It took a long time to sort out the reason, because she appeared to be at an excellent school, which was concerned to help her achieve her potential. The problem seemed to be with one rather strict rigid teacher, who was attempting to have her class learn in unison. She had told them that they were forbidden to try any further exercises in the English grammar book, beyond those she gave the whole class. When I asked Janice to try the last one in the book, she was horrified; 'That is for the end of the year', she said, which was in seven months' time. But with my encouragement she tried, and did it perfectly in a few minutes, as well as the five previous ones. Clearly, she should have been working at a much higher level. The school was informed, tactfully, the teacher did recognise Janice's exceptional ability and present frustration, and gave her appropriate work. And the temper tantrums stopped.

Correction

You can correct a child too carefully. Who wants to give his 'all' in a story, only to be constantly put right for grammatical mistakes? Bright children have a need to explore ideas, rather than simply record information. They're much keener to learn when there's an element of investigation in their learning. Your genuine enthusiasm for his stumbling success is much more encouraging than putting him right.

ENCOURAGEMENT TO LEARN

A child can either learn in fits and starts or make smooth steady progress; it depends on what's being learned and on how it's taught. For instance, if you're trying to teach a toddler how to read, but the baby keeps interrupting, the toddler won't remember his learning as well as if he had no interruptions. But if he has some reading practice just before going to sleep, so that there's a long time without disturbance, his learning 'takes hold' better. Parents can help their children to good learning, both at home and in school, by using the following suggestions.

Encourage the will to learn

All children start off by wanting to learn. But if this will seems to be lacking, try to find the cause. Check on matters such as feeling unhappy with a teacher, friends not being nice, or insecurity at home, any of which can affect a child's willingness to learn. Check on the way the school is teaching – has your child any special problems with the methods they use?

Try to get your child's progress into perspective. Sometimes parents, who are so closely involved, become worried over what they feel is poor learning, though the child may really be doing very well. When our first child was barely toddling, for example, my husband and I were very concerned about his slow progress, as we saw it, in talking. So, one day we put our heads together and counted all the words he could say. They totalled 50 – quite a lot really – and we never worried about his talking again.

Rewards

Rewards can be a very effective way to encourage children to learn. Parents who think positively, who use praise lavishly (where it's justified) and who give treats (small) for extra effort will probably have a child who feels happy about learning. Sarcasm and punishment are well known to psychologists as being very much less effective than praise (which is deserved) in helping children to learn.

Feedback

Good feedback from work done well is warmly satisfying. It also helps a child to set his sights at the right level; he can then avoid both certain failure from work that's too hard, and too quick a success from work that's too easy. A child draws conclusions from each learning experience, so that his approach to new learning depends very much on what's gone before.

Both success and failure in learning tend to perpetuate themselves. Parents can give a child a feeling of success, and so positively enhance his will to learn more. Take a simple example of a toddler learning to carry a cup of water without spilling it. If the cup is too full for him to manage at his age, he'll get negative feedback in the form of water on the floor and of parental dismay in his ears, which makes him feel bad. When the water's at a level he can manage and the job is carried out to perfection, he'll receive the praise due to him, and feel good about it.

Family feeling

All families exert a certain amount of influence on their members, and much of it is in the form of example by the parents. When parents are active and keenly interested in life around them, then the probability is that their children will be the same. Show your children, by your example, that learning gives a lifetime of pleasure, and that as a way of life it's worth following. It is vital to take part in learning about things along with your children, so that they don't feel learning is only something for children, to be forgotten when they grow up.

Flexible learning

The best kind of learning is flexible and adaptable, so that the lessons learned in one situation can be applied in another. This transference is something that bright children are particularly good at. One winter's day, a bright six year old who had learned at school that water expands on freezing, froze some in a plastic bottle to stretch it – and it worked.

Old learning can get in the way of new learning when it's not appropriate. When children change schools, for example, and have to learn another method of arithmetic, they'll take longer over this than they did with the first method. Old learning that becomes really entrenched is called habit, and becomes more and more difficult to shift as it becomes embedded.

Action

Everyone has to take an active part in their own learning, whether by sand and water play, by talking about things or by mixing chemicals. The least efficient way of learning anything is to listen to someone else telling you about it – like a lecture. Whenever you can, think of ways in which your child can learn by doing something. For example, don't merely describe an electrical circuit, but set one up together.

Little children have to learn that when they put more effort into learning, they are more likely to be successful. It's no use, therefore, insisting to little children that they have to try harder at school to bring up their standard of, say, writing. The understanding will come of its own accord to some extent, though gentle encouragement is always welcome. By six or seven, though, most children will have got the message that they have to work to learn well.

As bright children get older, they usually become attracted to more complicated pieces of learning, like maths problems that they can really get their teeth into. They sometimes even use less capable children as markers, whom they feel they should pass. It adds a little spice to the exercise of their learning.

SCHOOL LEARNING

The key to providing suitable education for bright children in school lies in more flexible methods of teaching – methods more often used in primary than secondary schools. Team teaching, for example, involves a team of about five teachers to look after several classes of children. The special talents of each teacher are thus offered to all the children in the different classes, providing them with a much broader view than they would have had with only one teacher – an antidote to drudgery.

Infant schools sometimes use the village school system,

whereby five, six and seven year olds may be in the same class, just as they used to be in village schools. Older ones can then take care of younger ones, guiding them in school lore and helping them get ready for lessons or going home. It gives the older ones a sense of responsibility and eases newcomers into the school ways. It also reduces competition for places in the class and allows the children to work at their own pace – slow or fast.

My suggestion for children who are specially talented is a football team approach. Just as groups of the school's most skilled footballers might gather together on Saturday mornings or after school for a tutored practice, so should children who are talented in other ways be given the same provision – taken to other schools to form a bigger group. The same facilities are there for all subjects, and it would not cost much to have them available to all who want them. Those who lost interest would soon drop out, and there would be no need to pre-select children for any of this additional enrichment to their normal school curriculum.

In a more conventional age-graded system, parents and teachers have to work within the structure. One obvious choice for the advanced child in that situation is for him to jump a year. Alternatively, a child in a really flexible school (whose head is a wizard at timetables) might skip a class in just one or two subjects. This is more likely to happen in secondary schools, where subjects are treated separately, with different teachers and specific times allotted to them. Children who are exceptionally advanced at school may be able to join college classes in subject areas in which they excel.

However, even for very bright children, this acceleration through school isn't the best idea. It's much better to provide them with something extra to work at, either in school or out of school hours. Moving up to a class of children a year or two older, either for a little while or permanently, brings up the following three questions:

- Has he really got the physical ability to take part in games and activities with older children? If he hasn't, he may begin to think of himself as puny, a physical and (maybe) mental failure. His teachers may forget his real age and inadvertently confirm these unfortunate feelings.

- Has she got the mental ability to play with older children on equal terms? If she's always the youngest in the group, and she acts her age, then the others are likely to exclude her from their play, and it may make her feel bad.
- Is he socially mature enough to cope with being with older children? It takes quite a lot of effort to behave older than you really are for eight hours a day, five days a week. Would it be fair to place that strain on your child for the rest of his school life?

Many human aptitudes, though, are better developed outside the classroom than in it. Bright children can benefit greatly through contact and working with artists, performers, agricultural and industrial scientists, scholars, craftsmen and other professionals who are not primarily educators. As parents, you could suggest that the school makes arrangements with local colleges for bright pupils to go to a few classes, attend a course, or meet some of the lecturers for discussion.

It's not always money that is lacking; educational provision for bright children can be improved to a considerable extent within the facilities that already exist. It needs a fresh outlook, a real concern, a willingness to tinker with routine, to think sideways. Bright children need adult energy to help them now, for one day we will benefit from theirs.

All of these ideas, and others, can break up the lock-step of rigid formal teaching, where each child is locked by age or school-class into the same lessons, timing and homework, regardless of ability and maturity. Thinking around the problem can help to provide all children with the varied stimulation and regular challenge they need in school.

PRIVATE EDUCATION

Why do parents choose to pay, when most children can go to school free? Mainly it is to give their children a better chance of exam success and to direct their children towards the same outlook on life as they have. Every school has to be judged on its own merits, and parents want a great variety of things for their children, so it is important when looking at a school not to take anything for granted. The standard of teaching, the atmosphere, the size of the classes, individual attention, physical punishment, emphasis on sport, etc. – all affect the present and future life of your child, whether you pay or not. Private secondary schools, for example, often have the same size of classes as state schools. On the other hand, either type of school may take smaller groups of children for some lessons, so ask exactly how the school's teaching groups are arranged. If they can, some parents prefer to move to a catchment area for a good state school.

Teachers in private schools are often assumed to be of a higher standard, though all teachers are awarded their qualifications by the same system. However, teachers do naturally apply for posts in schools where they feel most comfortable, and so the kind of teachers who end up in private schools are more likely to meet with the approval of the schools' clients – the parents. I have surveyed teachers about their educational aims and found that there was no real difference between the attitudes of those in differently funded schools. In general they're not happy about compromising their educational beliefs, whatever these may be and whoever pays their salaries.

Schools that select by ability sometimes offer a somewhat limited lop-sided form of education, dedicated to getting most of their pupils through public exams. It teaches pupils to think in a compartmentalised way, which hampers creativity. The pressure to be successful in exam terms can bring emotional problems to some children, though many clever children are very happy at selective schools. They rub shoulders with children who are as bright as they are and who are as keen to do well. They're unlikely to suffer from a great deal of boredom, because the lessons are pitched at their own level. As you might expect, selective schools do get better exam results than mixed-ability schools – after all, the pupils are chosen for their cleverness – though the teaching methods are usually pretty conventional.

WHAT BRIGHT CHILDREN REALLY WANT FROM SCHOOL

In my research I asked over 200 bright children, aged from five to fifteen, what they would have liked in their education. Most of them were well aware of the style and quality of the education they were receiving and felt strongly about it. In general, they wanted a change of approach – in the style of education rather than the content. I had to conclude that there isn't a better person to ask about a bright child's educational needs than the child, whatever their age. Here are a few comments from the younger children, often said with some wry humour, in which they pointed out some aspects of their school lives that they found less than helpful.

Brian (age eleven) You spend four years in junior school persuading your teacher that you're a nice boy, but work ... no way ... you tell jokes and show how happy you are.
Wendy (age nine) If it wasn't for the ambition of the pupils, the school would collapse.
Sarah (age nine) If a teacher tells you to shut up, she tells you to go to sleep. Then you wake up when the bell goes.
Andrew (age ten) The teacher who screams about heads rolling is regarded as a twit. Teachers who regard themselves as respected are a pain in the neck.
Gillian (age eleven) Our primary school teacher was drunk on power; he could do anything, make anyone cry. I used to count the cracks on the ceiling, and had all sorts of games I could play while he was telling me how hopeless I was.
Kevin (age eight) A poor teacher says 'It's like that'; a good

teacher asks 'Why is it like that?'

Henry (age seven) You don't learn when the teacher's in a bad mood; you have to learn it the next lesson, when he's in a good mood. When I sleep in lessons, my head gets itchy. The one benefit of TV is that I don't go to sleep.

Robert (age eleven) A teacher decides on your grades. If you tell good jokes and have short hair, you're OK. But even if you come top of the class and the teacher things you're stupid, he'll continue to believe it.

Stephen (age eleven) Kids are dangerous things that mess up your school. Teachers are in competition with their classes, because there's all this competition in education.

And these are some of their suggestions.

What kind of lessons do you like?

The preferred lessons were long ones, where bright pupils would have time really to get to grips with what they were doing. They didn't like snippets of information being handed out to them, but preferred to see the pattern of learning. For example, a 12-year-old boy said he was interested in the principles of heat production, but he'd had to spend a lot of time learning details first. He felt he should have had the two aspects together.

They also wanted to take part in designing their own lessons, to know what they were aiming for, and how they were to spend their time getting there. A girl of 13 said her teacher often gave the class lists to memorise in history, which she found very frustrating; she'd really have benefited more from a broader approach to the problems of the period she was studying, such as an understanding of the era as a whole, and then filling in the details.

What do you think education should do for you?

The children saw their education as helping them to grow up to be well balanced and competent. They wanted their own values and interests to be respected while they were at school, and resented what they described as an over-emphasis on their intellectual development. Their description of what they wanted was often of a 'healthy' education.

Are you ever bored?

All children have times of boredom in school, but with bright ones it is sometimes due to the special ways they have of learning, which teachers aren't always aware of. For example, for most children learning a subject usually progresses from simple to complex, singular to plural, and in the 'right' order – right, that is, according to the school. But bright children sometimes skip bits of the process, so that while the teacher is explaining how to do long-division in the time-honoured manner, the aspirant mathematician has worked it out long ago.

Flexible methods of teaching can help here, so that a few children don't have to wait in silence and stillness for the rest to catch up; when children work at their own pace, time is not wasted in waiting. Children I spoke to often said that if they were able to explore more in their own way – under guidance – they wouldn't be bored. A 15-year-old boy said he felt over-controlled at school; he was keen to get on with the subjects that interested him, but he had to stick to what the teachers told him.

A few children said they were bored because it was all too easy. They longed for a really challenging situation with other children who were at their level, where there was a real chance of failure. One group of bright girls used to meet outside school hours to discuss ideas that their teachers felt weren't suitable for the class.

What kind of teacher do you like?

Overall, bright children want teachers to teach. Friendly, warm-hearted teachers are always nice to be with, but bright children have a thirst for knowledge, and where better to get it than from teachers? The most sought-after teachers were not the cleverest, but the most open-minded. The brighter the child, the less likely he was to be affected by the teacher's personality or style of teaching. The combination of a flexible school and a secure open-minded teacher is a sure-fire winner in a bright child's eyes.

How should schools be run?

The children came up with some ingenious ideas. Though some were concerned with mundane things like school dinners, others took administration seriously. Several suggested that having a single head was undemocratic; there should be a group of teachers at the top, with pupil participation at all levels to make the school work at its best. In general the brighter the child, the more independent of the 'system' they seemed to be. They put up with it (whatever it was) while they had to, but they really intended to change things when they got the power.

SCHOOL TALK WITH YOUR CHILDREN

Parents and teachers always have to work actively with a child to get the best results, and there isn't a better person to ask about the way her education is going than a button-bright child – at any age. This is particularly important for the brightest, because they are often having to cope with a greater educational load. This takes energy from them, even for those who appear to find it easy, so they need some extra attention to keep their spirits up when it gets a bit too much.

Talking when children are getting ready for school in the morning is usually pretty basic, concerned with what they need for the day and getting there. It is usually better to talk over the day's happenings after school. When it is made with care, your conversation can reach deeper and more effective levels than casual enquiries, and can ease your child's progress through school. You could try the following focused points.

- Is your child being helped to find out more about what he is interested in?
- If he has any problem, how are they being attended to?
- What are the really satisfying experiences at school?
- If your child had his way, what kind of teaching would

he prefer, and how does he feel about the approach his school takes to the pupils' learning?

- Does he feel that the marks he receives are about right, or could progress reports be improved somehow?
- What suggestions has he for improving the way that teachers and parent communicate?

Don't expect your child to be as enthusiastic as you may be over all aspects of her education.

Questions to ask the teachers

Here are some points you might want to discuss with the teachers.

- Talk with the teacher about the way your child seems to be getting on there.
- Ask about the possibility of there being something extra in the basic day's teaching for bright children.
- Talk about ways in which your child's interests can be developed at school so that she can perhaps specialise to some extent.
- Talk about ways in which her horizons might be broadened so that she develops new interests.
- See where she can share these new possibilities of learning with others in the class.

But don't try to push the teacher to give a lot of attention to your child's special interests when she may feel that, for example, her writing is more a matter of priority.

CAN SCHOOL SUCCESS BE PREDICTED?

The problem in trying to predict how well your child will do at school is that between a child's ability to do well and the fulfilment of his potential, there's a whole world of ifs and buts. It's extremely difficult to predict the development of an ability that hasn't yet had a chance to be tried out. For instance, Van Gogh, the painter, didn't have the opportunity to start painting until he was an adult, so it's doubtful whether anyone could have predicted his artistic success when he was a child; in fact, because of his innovatory style, he was never widely acknowledged as a 'proper' painter in his own lifetime.

Not all schools teach the same subjects or develop the same interests in children, even at primary level. I have visited a primary school, for example, where there wasn't a single musical instrument in the building. Yet, not far away, there was a very similar school that had over 30 children learning the guitar. The difference was that none of the teachers in the first school were interested in music, but the second school had an enthusiastic man who wanted to share his joy in the guitar. Needless to say, there were no talented child musicians in the first school.

Parents and teachers can only guess at future success from the way the child is seen to behave at the time. For example, there must be millions of boy babies who have had boxing or footballing careers predicted for them in their first few weeks of life. Sometimes parents really would like their children to grow up in a certain way, so they look for – and find – signs of it while the children are quite small. In this way, a girl can reach the age of ten, 'knowing' that she's going to be a nurse – well, she did bandage her doll's leg and she did stick a plaster on her brother's finger. And for many children, the predictions come true because they're not given much encouragement to consider doing anything else.

The best way of predicting future success at anything is to see how well a child can do it at present, and how keen he is to go on with it. The key lies in the child's own feelings about wanting success in that area. The five year old who loves playing with dough may not turn out to be a baker, but he might find so much satisfaction in handling shapes that he ends up as a sculptor.

There are psychological tests that are used to predict success for children. These are based on accumulated evidence from the way abilities have developed in many thousands of children; a child can then be compared with all this past evidence. But it doesn't always work. Every child is unique and has his own pattern of development, so that he may not fulfil the expectation calculated for him on the basis of all the other children's results.

Intelligence tests are made up in the same way (see Chapter 5 for more about IQ). They're very good predictors of success for groups of children, such as a school class, but can sometimes be wrong for any one child. For example, many children with only moderate IQs may not do well at school, but become successful afterwards. Maurice Sendak, the American writer and illustrator of children's books, was like that – a bright intelligent boy, but no scholar. He left school and worked at a number of jobs, until he found what he really wanted to do. Drawing was something he had always enjoyed doing and he was brilliant at it, even if the school didn't appreciate his talents. Now, he's given pleasure to millions of children – and also become a millionaire.

No matter how good the test, a child's results in it can be affected by what is happening on the day he takes it. The results can also be affected by: how he feels about taking

---

What you can do to encourage success in school

- If you put a high value on education, then your children probably will too.
- Try to see that your child has all he needs to work with and learn from, like plenty of paper and pencils and a corner of his own.
- If your child enjoys peace of mind, he's likely to learn more easily and do better at school.
- If you feel your child is ready for it, try to find him a good nursery school or a pre-school playgroup.
- Work along with your child's teacher for the best results for your child. If you think the teacher really hasn't got his measure, talk to her about your worries first. Teaching a child yourself, in contradiction to the way he's learning at school, can be confusing to him.

- Home emotional support is invaluable to a bright child who wants to do her best, especially if the rest of the class disapproves of a pupil who works too hard.
- Try to keep your expectations for your child in line with what he's capable of doing. The art is in getting him to exert himself without placing the goal so high that he's bound to fail in the attempt. Don't, for example, jump a reading book because you think you've got a clever child. Though he may be reading fluently, he may still need to take each step as it comes.
- It can be hard to do, but try to keep up your child's interest in what he is supposed to be learning. Nothing kills off the will to learn more quickly than boredom. Learning has to seem to be relevant to the learner for it to be taken in well.
- Allow your child to stumble in her road to learning. Watch yourself to see that you are not correcting every little error in her grammar while she's trying to tell you something.
- Reward good learning with affection and occasionally perhaps a present, but only where the effort the child has made merits it. Reward for no real effort loses its effect.
- Help children to learn how to learn from the beginning by following the ideas set out in this chapter.
- Encourage children to follow their ideas through, to persevere as far as they can.
- As parents, show initiative and interest in what your child is trying to do. Take him to museums and historical places, for example, to fill in the background to his interests. But don't overdo it; it's his interest that should guide you, not your keenness to be good parents.
- Teach your children to go first for the principles behind the material to be learned, then to fill in the details.

tests – scared or excited; how he thinks his teacher feels about him – loving or disapproving; whether he's feeling well or is harbouring a cold, and so on.

So test results for the same child can vary from day to day; furthermore they can also vary through life. A child's IQ, for instance, can change a lot over a few years, depending on his circumstances. Sometimes where a child's intellectual growth has been held back, for reasons such as extreme poverty or long illness, he can catch up when life takes a turn for the better.

Success in school is very often measured by the child's obvious achievements, such as passing exams. But there's so much more that's learned in school – like how to learn or think critically, and attitudes or values that perhaps can't be seen till much later in life. Memorising facts for exams is an irksome task, whereas discussion is much more stimulating. Consequently, some hate exams and give their teachers a false picture of their real potential, unless they have the kind of teachers and parents who look beyond exam success. Predictions for individuals are always something of a 'guesstimate', whether from the most complicated statistical calculations or from the most sensitive interpretations of a child's behaviour.

FURTHER READING

Joan Freeman, *Gifted Children Grow up*, Cassell (1991).

Louise T. Higgins, *Learning to Talk: from Birth to Three*. British Psychological Society, available from BPS, St Andrews House, 48 Princess Road East, Leicester LE1 7DR. A 20-minute audio-cassette with 20 page booklet. (1988)

Oxford Workbooks – *Beginning to Read, Beginning with Numbers*, Oxford University Press. Clear, graded, and well thought out exercises for a child to start with.

Seymour Papert, *Mindstorms*, Harvester Press: London, (1980).

WES *Learning to Learn*, (a complete nursery education course). WES, Strode House, 44–50 Osnaburgh Street, London NW1 3NN.

The Parent and Child Programme, Inexpensive, up-to-date books found in supermarkets and other stores, with good practical advice. Octopus Books.

Play Together, Learn Together, Melanie Rice, Kingfisher Books (1985).

Entertaining and Educating Your Preschool Child, Robyn Gee and Sue Meredith, An Usborne Guide (1987).

From Birth to Five Years, Children's Developmental Progress, NFER/Nelson (1980). (Provides detailed guidelines on when a normal child should be reaching different stages.

Sense and Nonsense about Hothouse Children, Michael J. Howe, The British Psychological Society (1990).

Toys and Playthings, John and Elizabeth Newson, Puffin Books.

USEFUL ADDRESSES

This short list is not all inclusive, but may offer pointers to other more specific organisations.

European Council for High Ability (ECHA)
Bildung und Begaben
Wissenschaftszentrum
Ahrstrasse 45
5300 Bonn 2
Germany
Tel: 010 49 228 3 02 266

Arranges workshops, conferences, publications, information centre, International Diploma on the Education of the Highly Able, international research, children's exchanges etc. National Correspondents in 25 countries direct enquiries to local facilities.

National Association for Gifted Children
Park Campus
Boughton Green Road
Northampton NN2 7AL
Tel: 0604 792300

Considerable experience of all sorts of clever children, and runs courses and holidays for them. Special expertise in counselling. Has many branches around Britain, or they can help you start one.

National Association for Curriculum Enrichment
Park Campus
Boughton Green Road
Northampton NN2 7AL
Tel: 0604 715000

Aims to improve teaching in schools for all children.

Royal Institution
Mathematics Master Classes
21 Albemarle Street
London W1
Tel: 071 409 2992

Runs two series a year for girls and boys in the 12–13 age group, one in the Autumn term and one in the Spring. They are run on Saturdays in London, and are open to all. Youngsters can join the Royal Institution as Junior Members.

International Mathematics Olympiad
Wissenschaftszentrum
Postfach 20 14 48
Ahrstr. 45, D-5300
Bonn 2
West Germany
Tel: 010 49 228 302 266

Department of Education and Science Publications
Publications and Despatch Centre
Honeypot Lane
Stanmore
Middlesex HA7 1AZ

Education Otherwise
Alternative Education Organiser
25 Common Lane
Hemmingford Abbots
St. Ives
Cornwall
Tel: 0480 63130

Advice and information on home schooling

The Potential Trust
Kingston Stert
Chinnor
Oxfordshire OX9 49L
Tel: 0844 51666

Runs summer schools and other activities for bright
children

Irish Association for Gifted Children
Royal Dublin Society
Science Section
Thomas Prior House
Dublin 4
Ireland

European Council of International Schools
21b Lavant St
Petersfield
Hants GU32 3EL
Tel: 0730 68244

The Schools Psychology Service
Can test your child's abilities. This tested evidence can be
useful in getting the local authority to recognise special
needs. Find it through your local Education Authority.

Cademuir International School
Peebles EH45 9JD
Scotland
Tel: 0721 29566

The only British school to specialise in providing an
all-round education for very bright children. They also run
summer schools.

British Dyslexia Association
98 London Road
Reading
Berkshire
Tel: 0734 668271

There are other dyslexia associations, so look up your local
one.

INDEX

INDEX

All Optima books are available at your bookshop or news-agent, or can be ordered from the following address:

Optima Books
Cash Sales Department
PO Box 11
Falmouth
Cornwall TR10 9EN

Alternatively you may fax your order to the above address.
Fax number: 0326 76423

Payments can be made as follows: Cheque, postal order (payable to Macdonald & Co (Publishers) Ltd) or by credit cards, Visa/Access. *Do not send cash or currency.*

UK customers, please send a cheque or postal order (no currency) and allow 80p for postage and packing for the first book plus 20p for each additional book up to a maximum charge of £2.00.

BFPO customers, please allow 80p for the first book plus 20p for each additional book.

Overseas customers, including Ireland, please allow £1.50 for postage and packing for the first book, £1.00 for the second book and 30p for each additional book.

NAME (Block letters) ....

ADDRESS ....

....

I enclose my remittance for _____

I wish to pay by Access/Visa Card

Number ☐☐☐☐☐☐☐☐☐☐☐☐☐☐☐☐☐☐

Card expiry date